TELL YOUR STORY

TELL YOUR STORY

Teaching Students to Become
World-Changing Thinkers and Writers

PAM ALLYN & ERNEST MORRELL

Arlington, Virginia USA

2800 Shirlington Road, Suite 1001 • Arlington, VA 22206 USA
Phone: 800-933-2723 or 703-578-9600 • Fax: 703-575-5400
Website: www.ascd.org • Email: member@ascd.org
Author guidelines: www.ascd.org/write

Penny Reinart, *Chief Impact Officer*; Genny Ostertag, *Managing Director, Book Acquisitions & Editing*; Susan Hills, *Senior Acquisitions Editor*; Mary Beth Nielsen, *Director, Book Editing*; Megan Doyle, *Editor*; Thomas Lytle, *Creative Director*; Donald Ely, *Art Director*; Jennifer Knotts, *Graphic Designer*; Valerie Younkin, *Senior Production Designer*; Circle Graphics, *Typesetter*; Kelly Marshall, *Production Manager*; Shajuan Martin, *E-Publishing Specialist*; Christopher Logan, *Senior Production Specialist*

All web links in this book are correct as of the publication date below but may have become inactive or otherwise modified since that time. If you notice a deactivated or changed link, please email books@ascd.org with the words "Link Update" in the subject line. In your message, please specify the web link, the book title, and the page number on which the link appears.

PAPERBACK ISBN: 978-1-4166-3152-1   ASCD product #122031   n11/22
PDF E-BOOK ISBN: 978-1-4166-3153-8; see Books in Print for other formats.

Quantity discounts are available: email programteam@ascd.org or call 800-933-2723, ext. 5773, or 703-575-5773. For desk copies, go to www.ascd.org/deskcopy.

Library of Congress Cataloging-in-Publication Data

Names: Allyn, Pam, author. | Morrell, Ernest, 1971- author.
Title: Tell your story : teaching students to become world-changing thinkers and writers / Pam Allyn and Ernest Morrell.
Description: Arlington, Virginia : ASCD, 2023. | Includes bibliographical references and index.
Identifiers: LCCN 2022027902 (print) | LCCN 2022027903 (ebook) | ISBN 9781416631521 (paperback) | ISBN 9781416631538 (pdf)
Subjects: LCSH: Composition (Language arts)—Study and teaching (Elementary) | Creative writing (Elementary education) | Critical thinking—Study and teaching (Elementary) | Storytelling in education.
Classification: LCC LB1576 .A6147 2023 (print) | LCC LB1576 (ebook) | DDC 372.62/3—dc23/eng/20220719
LC record available at https://lccn.loc.gov/2022027902
LC ebook record available at https://lccn.loc.gov/2022027903

32 31 30 29 28 27 26 25 24 23   1 2 3 4 5 6 7 8 9 10 11 12

To the children of LitWorld,

who show us how to love stories

TELL YOUR STORY

Introduction: "Tell Us What the World Has Been to You" 1

1. Create a Community of Belonging 11

2. Why All Forms of Storytelling Matter 37

3. New and Old Structures of Writing 59

4. Using Mentor Texts 79

5. Conferring and Assessment 101

6. Student Writers as World Changers 115

Conclusion: Two Key Ingredients 125

Acknowledgments 129

References 131

Index 134

About the Authors 139

Introduction: "Tell Us What the World Has Been to You"

Mara was 10 years old when we first met. She showed us the picture of her mother she carried in the pocket inside her skirt. Each day, when she woke up, she carefully tucked that photo safe and close back inside her skirt and, on the way to school, would tell herself the few stories she remembered about her mother and herself, "to keep myself company," she told us. Mara's mother had died a few years before. The nurse in the hospice center had taken this picture for Mara so she could keep a memory of her mom. We saw her frail face in the tiny square Mara held so carefully in the palm of her hand. Her eyes shone through her gaunt features. HIV had taken its catastrophic toll on her, but in that photo, it was as if Mara's mother knew that this moment would be the permanence she would leave, her legacy. Her joy and her sorrow both radiated and reverberated there.

Mara's story is contained in the photo she cherishes, but it's also contained in all the ways that Mara shared the stories: the games she played with her mother, the food they cooked together, and the way they held each other's hands on the way home from school and work.

Children hold fast to artifacts—both in their hearts and what they tangibly carry with them. These are the emblems of their story-telling lives.

We can teach our students to hold tightly to the power of story to sustain them and know we will always have it to fall back on when these feelings rush back long after our wounds have healed. Stories, lived and imagined, do matter. We must treat them with urgency and importance because they fuel our lives. We can ask, "What do you want your stories to do for you and those around you?" We can ask, "When you are lonely, what story is nearest to your heart?" We can get used to conversations like this, that don't skip too quickly to the window dressing of stories but, rather, get to the essence of how stories make us human. There is no better motivator to get our students writing than this one.

With this book, we share the power of story in writing instruction to develop world-changing students, writers who learn the power of writing by seizing the power of story, using this power to hone their skills and apply those skills across their whole lives. The power of story will help them become self-reflective, empathetic, and coura-geous learners in their classrooms and in the world.

Toni Morrison wrote, "Tell us what the world has been to you in the dark places and the light."

The darkness and the light are the lows and highs of the every-day. Story is not judged by one or the other, by its prettiness or grit-tiness. We are human more than we are good or bad or perfect or imperfect. This duality complicates the notion of the light. It helps us know as writers and storytellers that the light shines with shadows and that these shadows are another part of the light. As educators who care about our students, we can share with them the complexity of the human condition and how it is found at the intersection of both the light and dark. We can teach them how to use that realness, that authenticity, to become courageous writers and learners. This human condition—the beautiful, the challenging, the tragic, the miraculous, the complexities of how they live their lives, and how their families live their lives—is valuable and valued.

We have seen in the hardest of times how the power of story can connect us, in spite of loneliness and separation, across time and space, from virtual universe to virtual universe, even when we are most isolated from one another. The power of story can also hold us to our most precious sense of self, the understanding we have that we are not alone. By reading about others' lives, and writing about our own, we can help our students learn about who they are and who they can grow to be, flourishing with narrative as a tool for transformation.

We can help students learn that the everydayness of their lives is so powerful and will help them become lifelong writers, change themselves, and change the world. In children's stories, we should see the power of their neighborhoods, cultures, languages, and families as both courageous and ordinary. Toni Morrison, in her narrative storytelling, shines light on times and places that are grievous. Her writing shows the courageous and aching meaning of how people live their lives in a mode of storytelling that "comforts the disturbed and disturb the comfortable."

In this book, we will discuss ways to teach writing that shows our students the great power stories hold. In order to build world-changing writers and storytellers, let's

1. Create an environment of belonging.

2. Value oral storytelling and visual storytelling.

3. Teach story structure and value counter-structure.

4. Assess student writers in specific ways.

5. Uphold a variety of role models and exemplars.

6. Value student voice.

When we celebrate the value of human potential, teaching writing becomes teaching story. By centering story, we are putting back into prominence the number one best way to get all kids writing and writing well.

● ● ●

We have been working and thinking together about the power of story, in a confluence of research and practice, for 15 years. Our work together began with the creation of LitWorld, a global nonprofit organization we built to ensure that young people would have inclusive spaces to tell, write, and read stories that reflect the worlds they come from, the worlds they are fighting for, and the new worlds they want to create. We have created ways for children and teens of all ages to tell, draw, and write their stories when they had little else to comfort them. We saw them gain power as storytellers and then as writers. In Ernest's work as associate professor of humanities and dean of equity at Notre Dame University, he is extending the research that shows the long-lasting power of stories in young people's literacy lives. Pam delivers her work through programs, such as LitCamp and LitLeague, that center stories, whether they are shared by reading aloud, sharing texts and deconstructing them together with students, or inviting students to create, craft, and mold their own personal stories to make meaning in the world.

We have found that when children and adolescents see themselves not just as receivers of stories but as active participants and lead actors in communities and cultures that center their stories, their writing becomes powerful. There are new ways of braving story: authentic voice, resistance, freedom, transcendence. Canonized story structures contain unconscious and conscious biases against marginalized groups, and we can read these stories with a critical eye so that when students tell their own stories, they know they are putting their voices into a long yet imperfect tradition of storytelling. Our students come to know that they can share their stories in a multitude of ways that have an impact on the community around them. We read the past to write the future. We must work to make kids' voices louder, bolder, and stronger while they are in our classrooms so they are equipped to use them to change the world.

Together we can flip the notion of story back to our students: *their own voices will empower them as writers*. For this reason, we have to teach writing differently now. We must lead with the power of stories.

In this book, we will share principles and strategies to help students use their own stories, the stories they carry with them, to become lifelong writers. This is a different type of pedagogy that many in the education sphere are not used to, and it can be a significant adjustment to the English classroom curriculum. We advocate for this approach because we have seen the power that stories hold for our students. We have seen how teaching story can dissolve writing anxieties and resistance. We have watched students who previously didn't see themselves as writers fly through notebook after notebook, filling every corner with their thoughts. We have seen kids who lamented they didn't have anything to say grasp onto this story framework and learn to write masterfully.

Remember: writing is a technology, a technique. But even the most proficient writers can't use their skills if they don't have a story to tell. If there's no story there, then the techniques do not matter. When we unlock the stories our students want to share, they become more interested in learning the techniques to share them.

How do we generate writing ideas? How do we invoke a real audience? How do we use punctuation to emphasize themes? How do we show this character's flaws? How do we help students find their voice? All of these questions make much more sense in the context of a story. When our students know they have a story to tell, they have the intrinsic motivation to want to tell that story in the most effective way possible.

If you found a time machine and went to a civilization in some different era, when you got back to our contemporary society, you'd have an award-winning story. It wouldn't matter if you had great diction or killer command of the Oxford comma; your unique story would hold all the power to make you an incredible writer. Once you have the power of story, you naturally start to explore what tools help you share this experience with the world in a way that authentically and purposefully depicts what happened on your journey. A vast vocabulary or skill with grammar does not, alone, make great writers. Learning the ways vocabulary and grammar can aid you in telling a powerful story is how students can become world-changing writers.

Stories are empowering. Story itself is the engine of all great writing, no matter the genre, from narrative to nonfiction articles and poetry, from songs to the way we write social media. When people shape their narratives to an empowered perspective, they are happier and more confident. Stories are powerful because they build self-confidence and courage, build community when we tell who we are and what our core values are, and raise and amplify all voices to help people understand one another.

Stories are good company. When we lose ourselves in the stories we read, watch on television or the internet, or play in a video game, the best thing that can happen to us is that we fall through the words or images into the power of the story itself. We lose track of time. We laugh out loud or even cry. Whatever it is that happens to us, stories transport us. In times of trouble or boredom, they uplift us and carry us out of time.

Stories improve writing skills. As educators, we do not tend to connect what we mean by "good" writing with storytelling itself. We instead connect "good" writing to grammar and correctness, and when we miss this important step about the power of story, we miss the entire reason for writing and the greatest impetus to practice writing skills: because we want to make sense of the world and of ourselves. Because of this, our students often do not know why they are writing. They see it as a chore, as something they must do to please their teacher. All the skills of writing—the grammar, the polish, the vocabulary, the structures—come from practice. And we practice doing something when we love to do it and when we feel there is a pressing need for it. Tapping into story allows for the practice of writing to come naturally. In this book, we will lean into story as the heartbeat at the center of all great writing. Without it, writing is automatic and cold. Every genre, whether memoir, fiction, essay, nonfiction, or poetry, is grounded by the voice and heart of the writer; it's what makes writing come alive. If we center story as a priority for what we ask our students to do as they build their writing muscles, they will come to see craft techniques as meaningful and grammar and vocabulary as integrally important to their learning and growth. Their practice becomes encircled with meaning and purpose because they want their audience to hear them, what matters to them, and what connects them to one another.

Stories build inclusive communities. Remember that many students may be part of a particular group, community, or family who hasn't previously had the platform or the leverage to be able to tell real authentic stories about themselves, particularly in a school setting. If we can make that happen, we can shift these students' perceptions in major ways, helping them see themselves as more empowered in the world. Language itself is a large part of a student's identity and culture, and a storytelling community should center diverse languages and encourage students to write and tell stories in their home language. Learning the sound of diverse languages and seeing them written and featured in the room is good for all students.

Story is a wellness practice and an affirmation practice of someone's humanity. Being able to hear enlightening and positive stories about yourself involving people who you identify with is transformational. It creates a more equitable plane, a more polyvocal plane, where more people have the ability to narrate their own existence. We can begin to tell stories in dominant modalities that can help change larger public perceptions. It contributes to intercultural understanding. It can help humanize the faces of those we don't know. It helps subcultures or nondominant cultures resist oppressive structures. With story, we can share in a mutual humanity and soothe one another's souls. Teaching writing in this context is far more than how we learn grammar or vocabulary, although these things matter too. It is also about how our students can use writing as a wellness practice for the rest of their lives, a habit and a benefit to their entire emotional well-being.

● ● ●

In Chapter 1, we will share essential qualities of an environment of belonging to help every student see themselves as a powerful writer. The work we do as storytellers starts at the story of ourselves, but it is connected to our deepest sense of community. The work of storytelling moves us through the world, to becoming world changers if we understand that this practice is powerful and it's ours.

In Chapter 2, we will share how the forms of oral and visual story-telling are crucially important to the development of strong writing skills. We can honor the ancestors, ours and others', who have made story possible in this world and learn from them: from Indigenous communities that have passed down oral histories for centuries to diverse uses of language and conversation as tools and traditions to emulate.

In Chapter 3, we will examine new and old structures of writing that can help guide our students through the use of picture books, graphic novels, and art, how story is everywhere and accessible to all, and what structure can teach us about effective storytelling.

In Chapter 4, we will see how mentor authors can guide our students to learn powerful writing techniques, helping all students craft powerful stories and narratives with the thoughts, ideas, and techniques of those superb in their craft.

In Chapter 5, we will investigate assessment and conferring to help improve student writing, including how we can identify strength in story and writing that is inclusive and structured, so that assessment is more than grammar on a page but values the life-changing work of story.

In Chapter 6, we will provide ways for students to get activated with their own voices as young writers, from media creations to writing that will influence our students' power in the classroom and beyond, to become world changers themselves.

And in our Conclusion, we will share final thoughts and a call to action for your own practice, a reminder that you and your stories are also at the heart of what your students will remember and recall about you for the rest of their lives.

Writing instruction does not have to be held hostage in a literacy block; it should find its way into science and math, social studies, the arts, and physical education, from morning to evening. Story is the thread that runs through all of learning and life. We can increase writing and communication skills as scientists, historians, technologists, mathematicians, and more by centering stories. Each and every one of the prompts you will find in this book can be used at all ages and across all disciplines to boost your students' understanding of the power of story to amplify their writing skills. So, don't limit them to the 90-minute period you are focused on literacy. Literacy and writing should track everywhere.

This model starts with the question in every subject area: "How can every writer and learner feel a sense of belonging here to take a risk and share in one's most authentic voice?" and then leaps to "How as courageous individuals do we use our own writing to make the world the place we dream of?"

Storytelling isn't just awakening to the world; it helps us make sense of ourselves in the world, to find our voice and understand how we fill ourselves in the gap of what's missing in this world. Writing in our classrooms must be more than our students making simple marks. Teaching writing by centering the stories of our students' lives is to step into the worlds they author. Centering their story is to make sure our students will radically love themselves so they can radically love the world. Stories are our way to get there.

1

Create a Community
of Belonging

*When we create a community of belonging, students
begin to understand themselves as story worthy.*

In order to build a community of lifelong writers in our classrooms,
we must create the conditions that will allow for confident, courageous reading, writing, speaking, and listening, all the components
of literacy necessary for student writing to bloom. Our communities
of learning must be communities of belonging.

The stories most often canonized reflect only a narrow slice of
our world. Most stories held up to be representative of the human
condition are merely those that are white and male. In this chapter,
we will help you learn to establish an environment of belonging that
shows your students their voices are powerful, regardless of what
their story might be or how it differs from the books on their school's
library shelf. With a community of belonging, all students feel centered in the understanding that their voices matter.

We can create spaces where children narrate themselves into being by sharing their own stories, whether these are stories created out of their own imaginations or about the multiple cultural communities in which they participate.

The first step toward communities of belonging is reconceptualizing story. A lot of times students (and adults) don't think of themselves as having stories worthy of sharing. We have to shift the conceptualization of story—from something that exists in a book or on the news—to something for which the only prerequisite is simply living. To see your life as story worthy is not intuitive; asking our students about their stories communicates to them that they have one.

When you write or speak yourself into being through a story, you create an artifact that triangulates your existence. Others can see me through the stories I tell, and I can also see myself as others hear and respond to my stories. This two-fold proof of existence—I see myself and I am seen—becomes imperative when we attempt to foster belonging. One of the biggest challenges we face in education is a self-ability crisis, a self-loathing crisis, a crisis hinging on a lack of belonging deeply felt by our learners.

As educators, we must strive to remedy this above all else. At the end of the year, we hope our students love themselves and love their minds more than they did at the start. It doesn't matter if you've got someone with perfect scores on standardized exams if they look in the mirror and see someone they despise. The academy and a collusion of communicative infrastructures will send the message that our students should not love themselves, that they don't have anything to offer, that they are not worth much. We contend against these constantly when our students belong in a community. Offering your story to situate yourself as someone who is teaching, sharing with, and offering yourself to others is the ultimate antidote to self-loathing.

You can put an *A* on a student's paper, but it's nothing like 15 people reading their work with rapt attention. In a community of belonging, you don't just tell people they are worthy; you put them in situations where that is obvious to them.

Asking students to tell their story communicates two things. One, they have the talent to be a storyteller. It says, "I'm sure that you have a life that is worthy of story and that you have the eloquence, knowledge, and skills to tell it best/better than anyone." Two, it reinforces all they have to offer their community. A community of belonging cultivates self-worth, and self-worth cultivates world-changing writers.

● ● ●

After repositioning our students as their own storytellers, they will begin to look at the texts they read differently: through the lens of story. We can ask them, "How is this writer telling a story?" rather than, "How is this writer using an adjective?" The adjective is of course important, and we love those too: they are part of our toolkit. But if our students consume stories with the driving concern of the story-teller, we can help them unlock the *purpose* of that adjective.

In school we often associate writing with a chore that takes great effort, assuming writer's block and other assorted anxieties often get in the way. We begin reiterating the difficulty of storytelling at a very early age, preaching to our youngest students that there are land-mines everywhere we look: from the ways we spell words, to intricate grammar rules, to a daunting blank page.

In the classroom, we need to reset and realign our priorities to our larger mission. Our curriculum should not be full of the require-ments and conditions of good writing, the adjectives and so on, but the purpose of why we write. This environment is not made easily and is going to need consistent work and practice. We have to build a community of belonging where the environment is both challenging and also wholly safe. That is a hard balance for us as teachers.

There are 11 principles upon which we can build our communi-ties of belonging to develop, teach, and nurture great storytellers who become great writers: celebrate joy, actively listen, value wonder, prioritize creativity, welcome innovation, foster problem solving, be pro-empathy, hone routines, help students thrive, disrupt negative thinking, and celebrate every day.

Center Joy

Story rests on a foundation of joy. It doesn't mean that we need to be happy to write stories; it does mean that, in our community, people must be open to the collaborative nature of them. Joy must exist as your students tell, share, and receive stories. The singer Allison Russell has spoken of how the lack of positive inputs in a child's life can generate a false narrative of worthlessness in the child. A child who can tell their own stories can right that wrong, alleviate that sickness that is not who they are but belongs to someone else. Listening to one another's stories can soothe internalized traumas meaning that, while we may always carry them, "when we talk about them and sing about them and reduce them to a manageable size, then we can grow around them" (Scott et al., 2021).

Joy is never pure happiness; it is often tinged with sorrow. We love someone so much and so deeply that when they are gone we will miss them forever. We play with our child, knowing this moment will not stay. So many legendary children's and young adult authors have always known and understood this, from Margaret Wise Brown's poignant moments of transition in her seemingly simple stories to Walter Dean Myers and his characters' journeys into discovery. Many stories show us that sorrow and joy go hand in hand, but there is joy in talking about them and singing about them and saying, "I am here."

The educator Vivian Paley (1990), in her book *The Boy Who Would Be a Helicopter: The Uses of Storytelling in the Classroom*, said

> We must become aware of the essential loneliness of each child. Our classrooms, at all levels, must look more like happy families

and secure homes, the kind in which all family members can tell their private stories, knowing they will be listened to with affection and respect. (p. 147)

This is true for all ages, and joy is an instrumental part of that. With joy comes bonding, vulnerability, and communities of belonging. There are tangible ways to spark this:

- Create time and space for storytelling circles.
- Create a library of mentor texts that support the power of storytelling across cultures and languages.
- Give easy access to abundant resources for storytelling: technology and tablets, yes, but also notebooks with personalized pages such as
  » Photos of friends and family
  » Hopes and dreams
  » Favorite hobbies
  » Pets
  » Memories
  » Funny images
  » Favorite authors, illustrators, or musicians
  » Sports
  » Art
  » Collages
  » Journeys
  » Special moments
  » Favorite books or quotes
- Make words and stories into gifts: put small stories and seven-word memoirs into picture frames and place them around your room. Have kids make them for their families.

- Value free writing. Use it many times a day, even for a few minutes at a time, to get students thinking, to get their story muscles in motion in every subject area.
- Make humor and collaboration a part of your daily routines. The following prompts and activities can help with that.

Our Story Soup

Let's make soup together! This soup is a silly soup—it is made up of all the things we can find in the imaginary kitchen that is our community. Imagine you are making a pretend soup with your community and that every part of the community is something in the kitchen. Find things in your community to add to your soup. Does your community have a playground? Put it in the soup! Does your soup have a neighbor you love? Or a place you all cherish? Or a value you all hold dear? Put them in the soup! In the end, your soup will be made of all the parts of your community that you cherish. Try drawing this soup. What does it look like? What does it smell like?

A Smooth Stone

Find or draw a small smooth stone. Imagine that this stone began as a big rough stone that, after years and years, has been worn down to be small and smooth. This stone tells the story of our community. Just like this stone, our community is something beautiful. We can hold the stone in our hand, and we hold our community in our hearts. Tell the story of this stone through the eyes of your community. Who has walked on the stone to make it smooth? What kind of weather has worn down the stone over the years? What sorts of buildings have been built upon the stone that have weighed it down and made it strong?

"Yes and" Throw a Party

Take a moment with your friends, community, or loved ones to plan an imaginary party. Pick a person you all know, or a celebrity, and talk together about what the party would be like. Go around the group and have everyone share a detail about this party. Start each sentence with "yes and." For example, "At Oprah's birthday party we will have balloons." "Yes, and we will have cupcakes." "Yes, and there will be a petting zoo." Keep playing until you have planned an entire party. Talk together about the party. How did it feel to build something imaginary together? What did saying "yes and" do to your party?

Community Animals

Each person chooses an animal that they think represents the community. For example, your community might be a koala because it is very gentle. Or it might be a gorilla because it is very strong. Now, take the physical traits of each animal and combine them into one super-creature. It might have the wings of a bird (your community soars to new heights) and the hooves of a horse (your community is very fast). You have now invented a brand-new animal of your own!

Be a Deep Listener

Author and researcher Vivian Paley believed that a child is driven by story, that it is hardwired into them, and that if we tap into this inherent principle, we will unfurl their very core and essence. She argues that when they move from play to reading or writing later in development, it is all there: the building blocks of their own story and an awareness of their unique voice.

Paley modeled the distinctive ways she listens for stories: She sat with very young children and took notes on their words. Then she read the stories back to them and invited the child to select "actors," other children who would bring to life the simple and imaginative stories the children created.

The magnitude of that level of listening, of a child watching an adult take notes on their words and then having the power to bring those stories to life, is profound. We can do this work with all ages of our students. With older children and young adults, this notetaking can be more complex and recorded with devices or laptops. Regardless

of the method, joyful bonding and intensive listening means absorb-
ing, savoring, and honoring the lives and stories of others.

Paley's practices revealed the social and emotional importance
of play and storytelling to young children. As she wrote down the
stories as they were dictated to her, the other children would ask questions and exchange ideas, contributing to a classroom culture that
valued collaboration.

Symbols abounded in the children's stories that Paley recorded.
Sometimes a phrase would repeat in various stories throughout
the year, often various basic worries would manifest, such as being
left alone.

As students stage and act out their stories, they begin to understand the basics of the social contract: Do they belong in the scene
that they are entering? If not, what can they do to enter it, or how
might they take a different role? A group of children work through
basic questions of socialization as they all figure it out together.

The listeners set the tone of the storytelling environment with
open and curious communication. As listeners lean in and ask questions, they can spark creative courage in the storyteller, who is then
motivated and inspired by the invested receivers of their story. So
often we are rushed, and we do not believe listening plays an active
enough role in our work with our students. And yet, it may be the best
way to build that sense of belonging so that the oral storyteller can
first feel acknowledged and heard. And when the student goes to the
page or screen to tell a story, they have a learned memory of what it
feels like to be really listened to without judgment.

Some of the ways we can do deep listening include the following:

- Take notes when your students are storytelling. Carry a notebook or tablet or phone with you to every writing conference
  with your students (more on this in Chapter 5).
- Create a "listening corner" in your classroom, with recording
  tools such as notebooks with pens and tablets, so that students

can record one another, interview each other, and generally practice active listening.

- Post on walls and in online documents different ways for you and your students to practice deep listening: "What are you dreaming about?" "Tell me a story about your childhood." "I am here and listening. Tell me about yourself, your hopes, and your dreams." "What is one story you want to go back to and share again and again? Tell me that story twice."

Value Wonder

We are writing, talking, and imagining our way through our deepest questions every day we are alive. In every genre, be it nonfiction, poetry, a science lab, or a historical analysis, the writer becomes a storyteller: envisioning a question as they write and exploring an idea. If it's a book of many chapters or a cinquain, the writer is by necessity investigating, inquiring, and imagining.

This is why the community of belonging is so necessary for the student as a writer. They are not simply repeating a story that was told to them or jotting down the ideas you passed on. Our aspiration must be that we are cultivating the vulnerability that allows our learners to explore the world with their own words and ideas. Here are some ways we can build environments of wonder that lead to writing with freedom and assurance:

- Create a Wondering Window, where students can go and sit quietly to look outside or to simply feel there is a place in the room for quiet reflection.
- Create a Wonder Jar (on- or offline) with questions in it for students to use as jumpstarts for their writing, including
  - » Wonder about the world.
  - » Wonder about the sky.

» Wonder about the nature of humanity.

» Wonder about yourself: What are your forks in the road, your hopes and dreams?

» Wonder about your home language: What are the origins of words you use or love?

- Keep a Class Wondering Journal. This can be online or offline. Each week, assign students a day to create a wondering prompt for their classmates.

- Establish Wondering Partners. Each week assign students in partnerships to work in wondering partnerships and react to each other's ideas with a wondering stance: "I'm wondering what made you write this." "I'm wondering where this idea came from." "I'm wondering what you could do to expand on that idea."

- Use open-ended questions or wondering-centered questions when conferring with students:

» "What are you thinking about right now?"

» "What are you wondering about?"

» "What surprises you?"

» "What are you observing that you have a question about?"

Prioritize Creativity and Value Student Innovation

Creativity and innovation happen in every step of the writing process. If a plot is why things happen or why events happen in the way that they do, then discovering that reason is a creative, innovative project. Describing a scene that captivates the reader is a creative activity. The details need to be chosen, and a new world needs to be created. Innovation and creativity are intrinsic to that process.

Give your students a list of simple descriptions and have them make the descriptions as dramatic as possible. For example, "The grass is green and soft" could become "The grass was a bright green, and it felt soft like a bed" or even "The blades of grass were glowing and green under the sun. Touching the grass felt like touching the softest silk."

The difficulty can come with questions that are too broad. If you simply ask somebody for a creative thought, perhaps they can summon one up, but they are much more likely to be able to tell you which animal they would add wings to if they could, or what their ideal bedroom would be.

Creative thinking is best inspired by prompts, but there is a fine line between guidance and prescription. Let the prompts you give your students encourage their creativity. Do not judge them when they are silly or serious, somber or surprised. In order to create a community of belonging, we can share ways of experiencing the power of writing without judgment. Let the stories flow. Prompt students in the following ways:

- Envision a world of peace. What would it look like or feel like?
- What would school be like if you could tell a new story about it?
- Imagine you go on a trip with magical powers to help you get there faster or to fly there, and write or tell about it.
- Imagine a beautiful country where the laws were made by children or teens.
- Use alternative materials to tell a story (e.g., a paper collage, chalk, pencils).

Here we encourage you to let your students guide the way as practitioners of writing. Create and innovate and change as they go. Our students are bursting with ideas, and writing should be a vehicle to help them express all that. They are constantly innovating both language and ideas. Let's center that in our classrooms by valuing the magic of innovation. Here are some ways to do that:

- Create a Maker Space in your classroom, providing tools, materials, and resources for building and creating.

- Create an Innovation Hub in your classroom with small notebooks or tablets available for students to borrow and use as portable idea collectors.

- Ask students to do a Build a World activity, writing and sketching what they see as innovations that are necessary for improving our world—and don't underestimate the great ideas of your youngest students!

- Have students redecorate their classrooms to make them more conducive to writing, such as bringing in table lamps, decorations, and twinkling lights or creating cozy nooks and corners for authentic dialogue.

- Invite students to challenge each other and themselves by putting together a few seemingly unrelated ordinary objects they see around them and then writing about how they can change the world with those objects.

Become Problem Solvers

Storytellers and children have something in common: they are constantly trying to problem solve and make sense of a very complicated world. We cannot underestimate the power of storytelling to actually help our students *solve problems*. All day long we are narrating our lives. We are telling and retelling our stories to ourselves, saying, "This is who I am," or, "This is who I want to be," or, "This is who I never will be again." We are complex, contradictory, and multilayered. Storytelling can and should be that way for children from the beginning. As we watch children play dress-up, they are exploring roles, patterns, behaviors, relationships, communication styles, and general ways of being. Our own children spent hours building forts from the couch, taking turns in "who do you want to be today?" and changing and rechanging the story as they went.

With writing, we tend to be far more rigid in the way we encourage our students. We see writing as linear and storytelling as finite. What if we learn more from children and really watch them at play? They are not linear. They see worlds we cannot see. Their minds are expansive, ever-creating, ever-changing. We can explore this notion of writing as problem solving by reorienting the way we present writing to our students. We can

- Establish time for writing as time for problem solving. Ask students to list three challenges they are trying to solve in an everyday way. Then have them write a story for 10 minutes as if by the end of it they would have solved that problem.
- Next ask them to do the same for a community problem.
- Now ask them to do the same for a world problem. Ask them to tell the problem and solution as a story and see where it takes them.

Have students work in pairs. Write or draw a problem they think is worth tackling in the school. Now ask them to storytell their way through it. Start with a vignette: something that shows how the problem affects the children in the school (e.g., not enough time for lunch or kids feeling stressed). In part two, have students solve the problem with a new story: How would their school feel after they use their own stories to solve a problem? Even more broadly, you can have students envision a new world of school without that problem in it. Tell it through a story.

In one middle school classroom, the students were asked to rush from one period to the next, and they wrote and shared about how they felt pulled quickly in a million directions and that this approach made them feel disconnected from each other and hurried in their learning. They proposed that during the day there should be two reflection points where they could pause and reflect and write in a journal or simply meditate briefly in silence. They wrote and shared about how this practice helped them calm down, and notice their surroundings more, and be prepared for their work in the next period. Finally, they told the story of a new time at school, where the halls felt more tranquil and where their entry into the next class felt more purposeful, exciting, and refreshed.

Make Pro-Empathy a Core Value

A pro-empathy classroom environment is really about empathy for oneself, as well as for others, for one's own steps into one's own identity and sense of belonging. If every student considers themselves a storyteller and writer, and they are forgiving and loving to themselves, these habits will translate to others too. In a pro-empathy classroom, our students are always looking through the lens of story to ask, "Who am I, and who is that person next to me?" No one should be a stranger in a community of belonging. Pro-empathy means we actively work around how we can inhabit the worlds of others and how we can take tender care of ourselves. Literacy and the power of stories show us how to empathetically take others' perspectives. Each book and each story we read is an author attempting to make the world stronger by writing their way into an understanding of the human spirit and the human condition. Story is what makes us human, after all.

A story shared can provide insight into other people's minds, struggles, lives, ambitions, and patterns of thought. A story, whether it is about a dragon or a historical figure, has a point of view, and that point of view is different from the one that the reader has had their whole life. It's dangerous to only know one story, as Chimamanda Ngozi Adichie (2009) says in her TED talk "The Danger of a Single

Story." "The single story creates stereotypes, and the problem with stereotypes is not that they are untrue, but that they are incomplete. They make one story become the only story" and "flatten" one's multifaceted experience (13:14).

A story provides a look at the world around you, and it provides another lens for you to use. The more lenses you acquire, the easier it is to switch to a new one and consider what the people around you may be experiencing.

Empathy is the ability to feel for another person, to feel their pain and, through that feeling, do something. A story can ignite and maintain an empathetic perspective in our students.

You can ask your students to do the following:

- Write letters back and forth to each other with partners to "introduce themselves" (even if it's midyear). For every age, this is so powerful and can be done multiple times across the year. "Let's reintroduce ourselves to one another. How are we changing and growing? Share about yourself anew with a partner." Recently, we listened in on one such conversation where students were writing back and forth to one another, and one 7-year-old said to the other, "I used to be afraid to talk in class, but now I'm not. I learned how to smile with my eyes. And I've become a big sister, so now I am really different!" There are, within each of these opportunities to "reintroduce" oneself, layers upon layers of story possibilities to draw from to write even more.

- Invite your students to write a letter to themselves in the future and a letter to themselves in the past.

- Ask your students to select a character from a book they've read or that you've read aloud to them and write about their experience from a first-person perspective.

- Write a letter to a character in a book, expressing your feelings toward them and what you might do to help and support them.

- Share a variety of genre options with your students (including op-eds, poems, social media) and invite them to write what they would do to help a fellow student. What would they say if they could reach out and really affect the life of another person?

- Invite students to take the role of a character in a book who is hard to like and put themselves in that character's shoes to write from that first-person perspective. A pro-empathy classroom is hard work; it's not only the easy-to-understand person who needs our empathy; it is those whose actions may be most unfathomable to us. Response to literature can help practice pro-empathy.

Create Story and Writing Routines

In order to thrive, our students need encouragement, affirmation, their voices centered, and the necessary resources to make writing and story a regular routine. We cannot expect our students to thrive with occasional writing opportunities or when writing appears only as an evaluation tool. The room must be alive with routines for writing. Routines are a linchpin of creativity. We each have internalized our own writing routines, but our students need them clarified and clear so that they can practice them.

Daily Writing

Build a daily calendar that calls out writing as sacred time, at every grade level, and not just the thing we tack on or take for granted. But let us also make sure writing becomes ordinary and common as our daily bread. Writing has to be valued yet also so ordinary that our students come to see it as a practice that is as essential as breath. Across the content areas, this practice can help our math, science, and social studies teachers see storytelling and writing as more of a regular constant in their classrooms too. For example, we can be on the lookout for story in science—both in terms of the people who have made inventions that have changed the world and also the story of the inquiry itself. When students are doing lab work, give them an inquiry notebook to write stories of the wonderings they have and the discoveries they make.

Writing Tools and Inspiration

Share with students abundant materials and resources for storytelling and writing in every subject area, not just technology (although yes to that). Remember that writing comes in different forms and different practices: notebooks, sticky notes, varieties of pens and pencils, and opportunities to sketch and draw. Robert McCloskey wrote *Make Way for Ducklings* by putting some ducklings in a bathtub so he could study them closely and draw them. E. B. White went out to his barn and sat there looking closely at spiders, taking notes on their habits, to write *Charlotte's Web*. Langston Hughes listened to jazz intently while writing his beautiful poetry. All of these are tools for writing and learning. Technology is not our only way into the world of teaching writing.

Provide access to small notebooks, sketchpads, and music to inspire the writing life in every student. Let's have our students know that writing happens in real conditions with many inspirations. Students can also record their own voices on tablets or phones and practice the power of storytelling as a revision strategy: using the sound of their own voice playing back to them to help them refine their narratives.

Make available a wide variety of mentor texts: books, magazines, blogs, social media, poetry, nonfiction texts, memoirs, narratives, fictional short stories, and more as examples of fine storytelling in every genre. We must keep these mentor texts in places our students can look at them again and again and study them. There are great examples in the public domain that you can add to a shared drive where students can browse them. For those examples not in the public domain, we need to create a way for students to get easy access via a classroom library or individual mentor text sets they can carry between home and school (or access online).

Even in science and math classrooms, we can see the relevance of a variety of texts and show our students the authentic value of story. We can read articles about scientists and explore their stories of discovery. We can read historical fiction, narratives, and plays to explore perspective, point of view, and characterization in historical contexts. We can use the power of story to bring alive the people who work in STEAM fields and humanize their work and discoveries. The stories we read in science, math, and history are so rich, powerful, layered, and often moving. Story is what lies beneath what causes things to happen: human will and impulse, mistakes, triumphs, and the extraordinary resilience of the human spirit.

Community Norms

Create community norms that allow our students to work together to support each other, without you, so storytelling can happen naturally. Establish community norms at the start of the year:

- Ask students to define what makes a safe writing environment for them and then build a word cloud that is displayed in a prominent place. Regularly check in to say, "How are we doing?" and reset when things are not going as well as you want them to.

- Create "a compass of norms," where you invite students to create drawings and sketches of arrows that point toward their hopes and dreams as learners in a safe and collaborative community. Hang them up or add them to a shared drive so students can tap into them when partnering up with one another.

- Decorate "storyteller commitments" banners about ways to honor one another's privacy, dignity, and sense of safety and hang them prominently so students are inspired by one another's ideas.

- Give regular short, fast assignments for writing (not just the long essay forms or memoirs). Short bursts of storytelling and writing assignments are powerful ways to help students flex writing muscles. Ask your students to write for 12 minutes at home, tell a story to a family member for six minutes, record themselves for four minutes telling a dream story, or revise only the first line of their writing tonight.

- Set up systems for deadlines that the community can get behind and that are not just about submitting finished work. Find reasons to celebrate, such as "We will have four writing celebrations a year, and here are the dates" or "After our revision process, we will do a revision share on x date."

- Create time for partner shares and other ways for your students to check in with others and you. They cannot be thriving unless they are getting regular feedback, even something as simple as an emoticon on a daily basis or a personal note once a week. If your students are writing every day, not all that they write will be submitted as a final product. Assume there will be lots of drafting and writing that doesn't get converted to a final piece. These writings and exercises also need affirmation; we all need that.

Help Students Thrive Independently

A student begins to thrive independently through their writing when they learn to convert their ideas into written, drawn, or spoken language. The next step after that is learning to use their voices differently for different people, whether they're writing a letter to the mayor or a fantasy story. It's important to have time every day to select topics, research them, revise them, edit them, and share them willingly and with one's own self-driven purpose.

This all relies on having reading and writing sponsors who model independent writing so that the student can begin to try it themselves. Routines mean our students can hold those independent skills and try them again and again. Writing takes time.

When a student is on the trajectory of learning lifelong literacy skills, they start very much as a receiver; they are read aloud to, and people tell them stories. The skills of learning how to read, how to write, and how to share one's own ideas helps them move toward what it means to be thriving independently as writers.

Thriving independently as a writer and author is having command of one's own voice, writing across multiple genres, and being able to express ideas in writing. Whether it's a letter to a grandparent or a memo to the mayor, thriving independently in writing means something needs to be said and you have the power and authority to say it. Thriving independently in terms of voice is bigger than just the writing—it's multimodal, and it means you have an independent thought or idea and you're willing to share it and jump into conversations. Our student writers can take increased responsibility for their own learning in every subject area and become people who, down the road, will be that kind of sponsor for others and ultimately help others thrive too.

For these reasons, let's commit to creating time at least three times a week for structured independent writing (SIW). We can do this during an ELA block or in any subject area, even if we give it 10 to 15 minutes three times a week. You can even plan with your colleagues to share the responsibility: on Mondays and Wednesdays SIW happens in ELA, and on Thursdays it can happen in a subject-area class such as science or social studies. Let students know this is the time for them to explore story in writing and oral storytelling too. The following pages should help you envision how you can make this happen, and the simplest way is to use the prompts we provide. Let them be featured on- or offline in a central location so that, during the SIW time, your students have access to lots of ways to begin. Each week, let your students know there will be a time for audiences to hear and read their writing, whether it is their fellow students, their families, or other classes.

Interrupt Negative Thinking and Turn to the Positive

We're always making sense of the world; we're always trying to figure out where we fit and who we are in this big vast universe of people. Storytelling and writing shape us; they give us a way to put ourselves into something and try to make sense of it. It can be the greatest tool for finding comfort, peace, and equilibrium even when times are tough.

Internal negative thinking around writing is profoundly disengaging and troubling for students as learners. What does it mean to create safe spaces for our students? What does it mean to encircle them with the kind of care that's going to enable them to be at their best and empower them to accelerate their achievement? How do we acknowledge that writing may be the hardest thing any of us ever do academically or even emotionally? Our classrooms need a sense of mindful balance and a powerful core value of celebrating one's own ideas in order to write well and learn well. We cannot create easily when we feel uncertain, insecure, or fragile.

There are three common reasons why negative thinking finds its way into demoralizing our students and making it hard for them to write at all. Writing often brings out the most negative thinking in all of us but especially in students who have been told their handwriting is not clear, their spelling is not perfect, or their grammar is confusing. So they may enter your classroom already in a mindset of negative thinking. The first reason for negative thinking is what we see first and based on rules: the student has not internalized or mastered aspects of the most visible aspects of writing. This is one hurdle to tackle, and it's not small.

The second reason negative thinking finds its way into students' minds is the sense that they have "nothing to say." This is a common refrain in our classrooms; students will often start the year with this mindset. We have to work to help our students remove these two obstacles because they will never write well if they don't write enough! The refrain often comes from a lack of practice with accessing prompts from which to write (which is why all the prompts you find in this book are designed to keep them easy and simple to use: so that you can share them regularly with your students to help them get into that groove).

Third is that writing causes anxiety; staring at a blank page or a blank screen just naturally brings that forward (try it yourself). No matter how many books or articles we have written, as authors we have the same feelings when we begin a new piece. Yet we have trained ourselves to be comfortable with that discomfort; we know it will pass if we push through.

Here are some ways we can turn the corner on our students' negative thinking:

- Set up rituals for storytelling and writing that involve sound, such as background music, and get input from your students about what forms of music will feel the most soothing and encouraging as they write (or allow them to use headphones to make their own musical choices if this is possible).

- Use sound as a way to start and end your writing time each day (e.g., chimes or a predictable musical note).

- Establish a meditation moment to begin your storytelling or writing routines each day, created by your students. Even a simple moment of silence can help students transition into a more reflective state of being.

- Show students an image that feels reflective and peaceful.

- Invite students each week to be responsible for beginning and ending the writing time with a ritual or practice they create.

- Create practices that interrupt negative thinking with positive and affirmational optimism. Hang up motivational quotes and use different types of inspiration.

- Self-kindness and self-empathy are a huge part of storytelling practice and writing routines. Talk honestly with your students about this, and invite them to notice and be aware of when they are being critical of themselves and turn that narrative around toward self-care and empathy for oneself. Talk about this when you come back together at the end of a writing period. We have worked with children and teens who live in the world's most challenging and compromising environments. Their days are full of struggle and challenge. It would be easy for them to see themselves as never getting a leg up. But when we ask them to turn the empathy toward themselves, we see transformations. Our student Moses said, "I was the lonely deaf person in my class in my home country. I thought I could not do anything the others could do. When I started to give myself empathy, I realized it was even more than that. I could give myself courage, because I did not realize the others did not have to struggle as I did, and this was not a limitation; this was my superpower."

- Set time to discuss "what to do when" writing block happens due to fear of spelling incorrectly, not liking their handwriting, feeling that they don't type fast enough, or other situations. Don't brush past these issues; they are a big part of why students often will go to great lengths to avoid writing.

Celebrate Every Day

We often talk about the "serious joy" that is sometimes forgotten in our anxiety about meeting standards, fulfilling a checklist, or addressing skills. But we learn to do well what we love to do. And the spirit of who taught us flows through us. This all adds up to serious joy. It's not lighthearted, but it's full of heart. It's the strongest pulse we need to do things well.

What we love, what we truly love, and what we remember and long for, we go back to again and again: baking Aunt Rita's cake, remembering the taste of it, remembering her. Jumping rope because our grandmother taught us how. Flipping the tortilla on the stove and seeing our father's hand turning it. The celebration of work is about reveling in those precious moments. Writing is hard. We need to celebrate it. We need to celebrate the small steps when a student has opened up to the power of their own voice. The celebration must be continuous, small and big, everyday, as everyday as the smallest routine.

Here are some ways to celebrate writing together:

- Put regular "power of story" rally days on your school calendar. Have students select one line from their writing (at every grade level and in every subject area) and share them online or over the loudspeaker each week. Have something special for dessert in the cafeteria on these rally days!

- Make stickers that say "Power of Story" and give them out once a month, and on these days have students know that they can stop each other or their teachers to ask for a 30-second story. Everyone should be ready to be asked!

- Invite a children's book or young adult book author to join a video call and talk about their own storytelling journeys.

- Once a year, host a "power of story" finale and share online or in person the results of a year of writing and storytelling.

To build a community of lifelong writers in our classrooms, we must show students what it looks like to belong. Fostering belonging with joy, active listening, wonder, creativity, innovation, problem solving, empathy, routines, interruptions to negative thinking, and celebrations reiterates to students that they are story worthy. We must promote a community of belonging that problematizes anything or anyone in our students' lives that makes them feel small, excluded, or undeserving. As our students begin to love themselves and see their potential, they start to share their stories with the world.

2

Why All Forms
of Storytelling Matter

All forms of storytelling, visual and oral, when practiced,
inform written outcomes.

It's important that we expand the definition of story from what a student would strictly read and shift to a living, breathing way of communicating that seeps into every part of their lives.

Part of this reconceptualization is including **oral and visual storytelling**, including film and media in our students' understanding of story. New and intelligent technology design in classrooms can encourage young people to use media as empowered storytellers, yet storytelling is the oldest and most powerful practice of humanity.

We have always told stories. Visual storytelling is the paintings, drawings, art, hieroglyphics, and sketches we share. The visual story is easily understood by even the youngest child. The type of storytelling we as teachers look for most readily is the written story, but in order for us to really see the power of storytelling as a tool for all our students, *we have to see oral and visual storytelling as valuable and integral* to our instruction, no matter what subject we teach.

Let's take a moment to consider the stages of writing development and how vital a role oral and visual storytelling play in that development.

How Writers Are Made

Talk/Listen/Talk Loop

A talk/listen/talk (TLT) loop is a back-and-forth exchange between teacher and student or multiple students. Make time in your classrooms to talk and listen back and forth with different activities.

- Do a "finish this story" exercise where someone gives a starting sentence. Then the group, often in a circle, adds and adds to complete the story. Record this story and listen to it as a group together.

- Create storytelling partnerships that last over time. Assign each week to each person as a listener or speaker. The listener records the story in writing or by audio or video recording. The listener is then given the job of retelling stories to the speaker each week. Let there be a discussion about how the speaker receives these retellings: Does it make them want to revise their telling? If so, they can revise/retell back to the listener, who can record the new version.

- Make the TLT loop part of how you encourage conversation in response to read-alouds and any other group exercise in the classroom. Ask your students to put the TLT loop into their recess play and anywhere else they are on their own without you. Have discussions with the whole group about how they talk or listen differently when they are more aware of these skills and roles.

Play

As we discuss frequently in this book, acting out stories—that is, manifesting a power over story through play—is crucial even if it's happening mostly internally. We must create a playful and open approach to story and the writing environment so that our students will feel entirely comfortable knowing that practicing, rehearsing, and drafting are all part of a storytelling process. Watching children at play is watching children at work—the work of the mind. We can learn a lot by listening and watching. Change the way you think about play; consider it the purposeful work of childhood. How can we make it central to our work in storytelling?

- Don't limit play to the youngest children. Give your older students a chance to play by building this into your schedule; call it innovation time or maker space time, and build storytelling structures into the play work your students do. Ask them to retell the experience they are having with a partner at the end of every session. Invite them to use tech tools to record their stories. Invite them to build, create, make, and draw to build stories and ideas for writing.

- Invite playful thinking by creating space for drafts of oral stories as well as written stories. Encourage messiness. Provide folders, different paper options, and multiple kinds of writing materials for all ages. Give students access to tech tools that are about building and creating.

Picture Making and Art

You see children naturally making visual representations long before they learn to write letters, but we need to be sure we value and do not discourage the older students from using visual techniques and effects to tell stories. It is no surprise that graphic novels are so popular. People of all ages love them, and they demonstrate the value of storytelling in multiple ways.

- Set up art stations for storytelling that bring out the different aspects of a story, including collage, montage, watercolor, and black-and-white pencil sketching.

- Use picture books and graphic novels as models and mentors for the storytelling and writing process. Share templates with comic strips and graphic novel boxes so your students can fill in ideas of their own. Show wordless picture books to all ages. Model for them the structure of these texts, and invite your students of all ages to deconstruct the wordless picture book story narrative and identify the arc of the story and the climax.

- Where possible, use cameras. Encourage your students to view the world through the lens of their perception. Ask them to take a photo that represents their best day, their worst day, their hopes and dreams, or their deepest noticings. Then tell a story about it or write about it.

Putting Words and Letters Together

Young children will seemingly put words and letters together at random because they are watching grown-ups as they write, type, or talk, and it is fascinating to them. Encourage them to tell a story orally as they go and, if you can, transcribe what they say to keep a record of these stories. For older students, record their voice as they type or write. Remember: what may seem fanciful and unclear to you is them figuring out how to put structure to their storytelling work.

The more messiness the better. We want students to feel power in making sense of the tools of language. They need to do this both in their speech and in their writing to practice the ways ideas and language form. Remind yourself that a child learning to walk does just the same: they get up, hold on, let go, and stumble forward.

We celebrate that imperfection; let's do the same when it comes to storytelling and language development.

● ● ●

As students begin to fumble through these stages of story development, creating an environment rich in audible storytelling is increasingly imperative. Oral storytelling develops skillful writers.

In native Hawaiian storytelling the word for story is *moʻolelo*, which also signifies history, legend, and tradition. It comes from two words: *moʻo*, meaning *succession*, and *olelo*, meaning *language* or *speaking*. We love how the combination of succession and language creates story. So much in oral storytelling tradition is about articulating our beginnings: How did things happen? How did they start?

In our own families and lives, we seek to understand beginnings. Beginnings matter. Origins matter. Whether they are mystical or real, magical or harsh, they are the beginning of us, of who we are and where we belong . . . or not. A writer spends a lifetime sifting through the mystery of beginnings. This is why so many cultures center their power around their origin stories.

How does it benefit our students to use oral storytelling? What is the history and cultures attached to oral storytelling, and how might students feel more connected to that history if they are allowed to sometimes tell stories aloud instead of writing them? Who are some famous storytellers who have tapped into the oral tradition, and how can we learn from them?

We have a unique opportunity with our technological resources to record and keep students' stories so that they can build bigger projects for writing in every subject area around them. We also have the opportunity to revisit history and retell stories together that need new narratives, welcoming a diversity of voices and the power of the untold story into our classrooms.

Stories also appear in casual settings, woven into the fabric of how we make connections to others and how we clarify who we are—past, present, and future. Our conversations are stories, and we are constantly improving our skills and adapting our stories to our audiences. Helping young people tell stories is good not only for their writing development but for their future communication skills in the workplace.

Storytelling can change our brains, can change our hearts, can change how we interact with people and the world around us, and most of all, it can change our self-perception: how we see ourselves in the world and how we express our power and compose the narratives that will shape our lives and sense of self. Receiving stories in oral, visual, and written forms can make us feel less alone, increase our empathy, and encourage us to use our voice to change the world. In a heartbeat, in a moment, storytelling can connect us with another human being.

Storytelling itself is not a monologue; it is a dialogue. It is communal because there is always an audience, even if that is in the nearest, dearest settings of home, where parents are telling stories of their great-grandparents to their children. Through story, our students learn what it means to be a member of a community, a family, a school. These stories may come in the form of oral, written, or visual stories, and they all go hand in hand. Our classrooms can foster habits of great writing skills by also affirming and honoring the skills of oral and visual storytelling.

When students use verbal storytelling in play and pretend, they create and inhabit a world that they might not otherwise have access to. "I can storify myself" is a mantra for ownership of one's own life and history. And as young as our students may be, they come to us already full of stories. Storifying oneself takes practice, and oral and visual storytelling can help our students practice it.

Ernest has said, "It is the stories we have been told that help one author of this [book] to understand himself as the descendent of slaves who were, in turn, the descendants of rich and vibrant ancient civilizations. The daily routines we set up for all the forms of storytelling are really about how we ask, and when we ask, for students' lives to be made visible." Let's consider the role of oral storytelling and what its purpose can be in developing writers, thinkers, and learners.

Oral Storytelling Develops a Sense of Audience

Telling oral stories is a method of cultural transmission. Telling stories is a way for audiences to participate and interact and consume ideas and feelings collectively. Telling oral stories is the first way we learn to connect with an audience. The youngest child knows what that is to take a deep breath and then exhale the stories of the school day. As our children grow, they often wonder where those stories have a place. By inviting stories each day, by asking, "What are your stories today?" and allowing space and time for those stories to flourish, we are helping our student writers practice what it means to connect with others and gain the immediate feedback from the audience, whether that is an audience of one (you or a writing partner) or a larger audience you've prepared for an oral storytelling event.

Also, let us consider the power of technology to unlock the storytelling power of all students. If we think back to times long ago, the only method of storytelling was oral. Anyone who could speak could practice telling stories. The challenges then were similar to some challenges today: creating compelling characters, coming up with an interesting setting, having some action and events that capture the attention of the listeners, and bringing it to a satisfying end. The beauty and magic of writing inside structures is that it enables us to tell stories across time and distance, and each time relay the exact same story. Performers traveling around telling the *Iliad* from memory served an extraordinarily valuable purpose of allowing ancient Greek society to have touchstone texts. These epic stories were known by all members of the society who heard them without an easy method for mass distribution.

Oral Storytelling Is Interactive and Group-Centered

The songwriter Allison Russell said the songs she sings are stories that help people connect "to a lineage of resistance and resilience."

Oral stories allow us to connect to tradition as a group and in real time. Oral stories have the wonderful strength of spontaneity and changeability. Up until they say each word, the storyteller can change it. Oral storytelling exists in the present even when the stories are from the past or are warnings for the future. We can ask our students to bring the stories their parents, grandparents, or an older sibling may have told them at home. Oral storytelling is of the moment, and each time that same story is told, it can be refined and changed. The audience is right there, and the group-centered work of storytelling gets a learner's brain used to the idea of on-the-spot revision and a fortitude for change when necessary.

When our children were young, we watched them play. When they talked to us and told us their stories, they saw us valuing their minds. Sometimes we asked, "What happened next?" though they usually didn't even need that much prompting. They were thrilled to be so in charge of their own narratives. Paley taught us how important it is to have children feel in control of their stories, even before they can write them themselves. They could decide who would be in their stories, and we would act them out. Imagine how powerful that feels for a child to know that the story they create, even from a young age, is going to come alive in the world and they have the power to make actors embody their story too. Social media is another venue for acting out stories: whether it is Instagram or TikTok or whatever will come next, people are hungry to tell their stories, share their stories, and see their stories enacted and replicated by others. And this makes them want to write. Writing seems more real and concrete; it's a way to make the multitudes of stories flying in the air far more permanent and historical. Story on social media is iterative, constantly evolving and retold by multiple tellers, in a similar way that play once was in our youth. This collective storytelling is innately communal; it requires an audience and interaction. When we tap into this communal understanding of storytelling in our classrooms, students quickly learn the ways their writing can influence their classmates. When students know their story has an impact and can change the world, their writing improves.

Oral Storytelling Makes the Classroom Audible

There are some really tangible ways to get students to move from oral storytelling to writing. You can also group students, where each person talks through their ideas and the others take notes. Everyone ends up with three sets of notes on what they say. The more kids talk and are able to hear themselves speaking about something, when it comes time to write, they bring those ideas with them. I try to get them to write it down. And I'll say at the end, "You know, I wrote down some notes and you should go write down what you heard." So there are a lot of different practical ways to move from modality to writing. Make the classroom an audible environment, where we hear student voices as we get to the art and craft of writing, because writing is essentially the modality of putting your voice into print.

The kinds of things we gain by listening to the audible voices have a delightful quality to them and make the final piece of writing so much stronger. There are very simple things that we can do to help young people understand—let's stop talking about writing and start talking about ideas and stories with conversations, notes, and pictures. Begin to break down the barriers between oral and written communication. When students struggle—with language or drawing or something else—change the modality of communication to help them find new methods to play around with big ideas.

Oral Storytelling Brings Out the Quiet Voices

There are many reasons why kids are quiet. There is a relationship between confidence and voice. If we make sure that we are working on confidence and learning oral storytelling in a way that feels celebratory and honors sharing small things, we can start to hear more of our students and maybe build their confidence as writers and learners too.

Kids get vocal if something feels personal and important to them, and we used to be in that category. Both of us were the kind of kids who never spoke in school. I mean, we never spoke a word. In four years of undergraduate lectures, not one word, either of us. But then we both started talking because, in each of our cases, we became activated by injustice. We started talking about illiteracy, poverty, racism, or sexism, and we both realized, "Oh, there's a lot I have to say."

We have to really anticipate our students' needs and ask things like, "Why is this particular student quiet?" We can make sure that the ways they get to share their stories aren't intimidating and anxiety-provoking for the quieter voices. By using technology tools such as podcast equipment or video, we can help our students tell their stories at home to a screen or into a microphone and then come to school ready to share. Let them tell their stories in all the ways that make them most comfortable. You can ask, "What makes you feel most comfortable as a storyteller? What might get in your way? How can I help you remove those obstacles?" Letting our students know how much we value their voices—quiet and loud alike—means we have to lean into the ways they learn best and help them use these tools to find their stories and share them most audibly and effectively with others.

- What makes you fierce?
- What is a big question you want to talk about?

- What gets you angry enough to want to change the world?
- What makes you want to speak up?
- What might get in the way of you sharing a story, and how can I help remove any obstacles?
- What would be the best way for you to share your stories?
- Use technology tools to record stories and then transcribe them.

Oral Storytelling Helps Us Practice Who We Are

Identity is fluid in storytelling and writing. We want to be open to the river of storytelling that can pour from any student and allow for stories and writing to flow. Ask your students questions and prompts that will get them to start thinking about who they are and who they are becoming as writers.

- I am the kind of storyteller who . . .
- I get inspired as a storyteller when . . .
- Storytelling makes me happy when . . .
- The person I most want to tell stories like is . . .
- I feel like I hear my most real storytelling voice when . . .
- Once there was . . .
- When I was . . .
- The first time I . . .
- The last time I . . .
- I remember . . .
- I wonder . . .
- My language is . . . and it tells my story because . . .

- My beginning is . . .
- End with the first line
- Start from the last line
- Animal characters that represent humor and journeying
- If I had a photo of . . .
- My ancestors teach me . . .
- My elders teach me . . .
- My ancestors did not teach me . . .
- My elders did not teach me . . .
- There were many times I . . .
- My story used to go like this; now it goes like . . .
- My story is now heard because . . .
- The only time I . . .
- When I was a baby . . .
- Soon we will . . .
- I used to go . . .
- When I was little . . .
- When we were young . . .
- The family I carry is . . .
- The history of . . . is the history of . . .
- The best time we . . .
- I speak in my own truest voice when . . .
- My favorite thing about you
- How can we use story to build connections within our own family? What do the stories we tell about our family members say about them?

- What do you love about a family member? Tell a story about them as a way to teach your listeners/readers your favorite thing about your family member.

  » For example, you love that your godmother is adventurous. Tell a story about your godmother that shows just how adventurous she is.

  » Option 1: Tell a true story.

  » Option 2: Write a fairy tale. Imagine your family member is the main character of a fairy tale. Write a story where your favorite thing about them makes them a hero. How does their humor, their hair, their adventurous spirit save the day?

Oral storytelling is not just rehearsal for the written language we hope our students will develop; it is a way to illuminate every human in the room and show them all the ways their words can come alive. In "Translating Oral Literature in Indigenous Societies," Sean Patrick O'Neill (2013) notes that in "the vast repertoire of human oral literature found in the anthropological record, it is the mischiefmakers who really stand out," who find their voice in a "deeply syncretic way, sometimes mocking tradition, sometimes respectfully paying homage, but without losing sight of their own sense of artistic vision" (p. 247). Oral storytelling can help give students ideas for how to play with writing "rules," giving them the oral language awareness to help them craft a compelling and unique auditory experience for the readers of their pieces.

Oral storytellers pause to create certain effects on their listeners. So too our students can begin to practice these pauses using white space and punctuation. In Jacqueline Woodson's *Brown Girl Dreaming*, she uses white space artfully, right from the very first page of the book. As you read, you can just hear an oral storyteller's pauses in those white spaces, making Woodson's impact all the more powerful. She plays with white space the way an oral storyteller plays with pause.

De-hierarchizing Visual Storytelling

We have a generation of young people who see literacy as both words and images. In documents indigenous to young people, they hardly separate the two in the way we would have 30 or 40 years ago. We have so many hypertexts like the internet and social media, graphic novels, or even kids watching the genre of Japanese anime with translations at the bottom—it is not unusual for young people to be able to connect written story and storytelling with visuals. To be literate today is to understand visual images.

The kinds of images that inspire young people consist of a really healthy tension between the professional and the homely image as an aesthetic. It's not always about "Let's go to the museum and gaze at Picasso and think about cubist art." It's also visual storytelling that is in real time and homemade. It's not as though we didn't have time to take it into a studio; that aesthetic is really powerful for young people.

The stories they make themselves on social media are real forms of art. A selfie is not necessarily some lesser form of art. It is in some ways the ultimate form of art because it's fast, it's in real time, and it's immediately communicative, often to large groups of people. As teachers, we have to be mindful of when and careful to identify where we are going to hold students to a specific aesthetic.

We want young people to see professional art forms and professional stories, but everyday art and everyday story are important components as well. Forty years ago, when hip-hop and graffiti were gaining prominence, people couldn't understand what the vernacular of professional art was, but they were seizing the day with street art. Keith Haring drew across walls with his "Radiant Child" images, telling a new story of an old city and changing the way we thought about art and a child's mind.

Keith Haring wanted his art to be accessed by as many people as possible so they could come to it with their own interpretations about its meaning. "The viewer creates the reality, the meaning, the conception of the piece," he said (Haring, 2010). His art became part of communities, seen in the backdrop of people's real lives, and his "Radiant Child" became inextricably linked to the lives of marginalized young people. Jean Michel Basquiat also did this with his vibrant, intense, critical, and groundbreaking work. When asked to describe his art, he said, "Royalty, heroism, and the streets."

It was probably 150 years ago when we came up with a term of *popular culture* and juxtaposed it against elite culture. It told us what was popular was more degraded; it was ordinary. Although we don't make that explicit contrast out loud now, we still imply it.

We aim to break that binary with our students and communicate to kids that both make up a tableau of different manifestations of beauty. We must be clear in our language to not distinguish professional story from local story, between the kind of a story that would make its way in between the covers of something published to the stories told in the classroom. We will remind them that they're all meaningful and equitably viable ways of communicating life and stories.

We want both ends—whether it's historic, contemporary, professional, DIY, filmed on a $40,000 camera, filmed on someone's cell phone, created with oil on canvas, or outlined with spray paint on the side of a truck. It's imperative we show kids examples of story that appeal to the way they encounter the world and is produced the way they produce it for students to see themselves as capable of creating.

Visual Storytelling Is Culturally Resonant

Visual art transcends language: anybody can experience it, and we can use it to promote storytelling at all ages. Visually impaired or blind people can experience art tactilely. There is no language knowledge required, and although other information can enhance your experience of art, it is not required for consumption. Even our earliest ancestors who did not have a written language can communicate to us through art. Drawings on cave walls, murals, statues, architecture, and what remains of it can be understood on the most basic emotional level even if we do not know anything about the artist or their time.

It's important and culturally relevant to teach visual storytelling more fully and to embrace its energy to guide our students and empower them for writing skills and development. In the Deaf community, American Sign Language (ASL) is a crucial lever to the power of story. Placement of signs and contextualizing the spatial nature of story are how viewers can follow the story through time. This is very different from written language and exceptionally important to Deaf culture. Consider studying ASL with your students, if they are hearing, to show them the variety of ways cultural and linguistic groups share their stories.

Images of our past run through our minds and remind us of people who are beloved, who have passed, and who are precious to us. Images may be concrete, like faces of people or the places we've been, or they might be more impressionistic, like the sound and smell of times past and the other sensory experiences that come to us in other ways. The interesting thing about the ways we teach storytelling to our students is how we tend to slip past the visual work we should be doing with our students to strengthen their power of story. We can give our students different mediums to try (e.g., pastels, watercolor, pencils, and more) and have them see visual arts as rehearsal and drafting aspects of the writing they do.

Art can help us communicate through time and space, and our traditions and styles are constantly evolving. We told stories through images for probably tens of thousands of years, and so it comes naturally. Keith Haring and others showed us we can tell stories on walls and put them into our environments. The Deaf community shows us that stories exist not only flat on the page or screen but also in vibrant three-dimensional forms all around us. Kids aren't just drawing; they are also seeing graphics in the world that they translate to their own experiences and from which they can build narratives. They see a story in these images more profoundly and earlier than ever before. So, when it comes time for them to share a story, they are already thinking visually. It is important for us to tell kids that this is a way into story.

Picture books, images, photos, cartoons, comics, and graphic novels show how the power of story goes far beyond print on a page or screen. Close study of the visual power of storytelling can transform writing and learning outcomes for all students. Some of the best visual artists of our generation are writing for young people now: Raina Telgemeier, Marjane Satrapi, Art Spiegelman, Bryan Collier, Sandra Boynton, Ezra Jack Keats, Christian Robinson, Peter Reynolds, and Yuyi Morales.

Marvel Comics, graphic novels, superhero cartoons: all of it tells a story. Let's bring these genres into our classrooms and study them. Jason Reynolds said he writes the books he never had as a kid but wished he had. His book *Stuntboy, in the Meantime*, with glorious drawings by Raúl the Third, shows us the way forward. We want a world in which there is visual and written representation of every child, and all stories are shown and heard.

Visual Artists as Mentors for Writing and Storytelling

The artist Jacob Lawrence created "The Migration Series," a series of paintings that tell the story of the Great Migration (Phillips Collection, 2022). His first paintings were biographical accounts of important people in the African diaspora. At the age of 21, he painted a set of 41 paintings of Toussaint L'Ouverture, the Haitian general who led a revolution of slaves to independence, and he made a series of paintings telling the stories of Harriet Tubman and Frederick Douglass. Because Lawrence also created picture books for children, such as *Harriet and the Promised Land*, he is a powerful mentor storyteller to share with students of all ages.

Our students can study these brilliant visual storytellers to give them a wide-ranging perspective on the power of story as well as see what they have done to transform the way we tell history. They can investigate the ways Lawrence told a story by using several paintings to take us on a step-by-step narrative through history. We can invite them to use him as a model to draw their narratives and replicate his techniques (e.g., details, chronology of time, powerful imagery) to talk about the qualities of great writing. Here we can see the effects of cultural transmission, the tools people use to tell their stories— such as color and texture—all of this contributes to mood, tone, and how stories are shared.

Picture book authors use a variety of mediums that are inspiring to our students and will help them bring out the different ways they can express themselves in writing. Four examples include

- Jacob Lawrence (montage/collage/oil)
- Tana Hoban (collage/black and white)
- Kadir Nelson (painting)
- Barry Moser (woodcuts)
- Garth Williams (pencil drawings)

Visual Storytelling to Write Well

There are many ways we can help our students practice visual story-telling and expand on their thinking to make their writing more visible to others.

Maps of the Heart

Have students draw a simple heart sketch (see Georgia Heard's seminal book *Heart Maps* for more on this). Inside this sketch encourage them to place all the heart-connected aspects of their own lives: their passions, people, language, memories, hobbies, interests, and more. Have them use the map to retrieve storytelling ideas, create stories, and share stories with their friends.

Self-Portraits

Students can create these multiple times across the year to examine how they grow and change. Give them different art tools to see what happens when they create their sense of self in different mediums. They should use the portraits as a jump-off point to create stories such as "Write a story of your portrait in the third person," or, "Tell the story of who you are now and who you are growing to become."

Sketches

Give your students sketchpads or online tools to do rough, easy drawings for ideas that are fast and simple. You can model these "mind doodling" techniques for your students to get the ideas flowing.

Murals

Use your classroom as a template. Put up big white paper across a wall and have colorful markers handy. (This is for all ages!) See what your class comes up with. They may reflect current events or experiences the entire class is working through and talking about. Let them know that this is a way to practice and rehearse storytelling. It's drafting in community.

Black and White Contrasts

Artists such as Barry Moser use black and white contrasts to create strong moods in their storytelling. Give your students charcoal or pencils to practice different types of mood and tone. They can study drawing techniques to see what Moser and others do to convey a mood, and then they can try it in their writing.

Textures

Keep a box of scrap fabric in your classroom and other different textural elements, including foil, tissue paper, or any found objects that might be easy to use in a collage. Let students play around with these textures and then write a story with those textures. Have them look at turn-of-the-century quilts and authors like Faith Ringgold who use texture in their books.

Cartoons and Comics

Share with your students of all ages the artistry and brilliance of Marvel comics, of Dav Pilkey, and of the variety of incredible graphic novels that have been published in the last decade. Show parts of them to illuminate the level of detail these artists put in to make a scene come alive. Your students will appreciate you taking time to value these forms because they may be the most common form they are reading outside of school.

Other drawing prompts could include the following:

- Draw five scenes that tell the story of your memories.
- Draw your family story.
- Sketch the image that comforts you when you are afraid.
- Sketch the image that makes you feel the power of love.
- Sketch an image that represents courage for you.
- Draw a timeline of your life.
- Draw a pencil sketch of a time you remember with great affection and then add color to a part you most want to remember.
- Draw symbols that represent you at every age.
- Draw a symbol that represents you as you really are.
- Create a scene that is the world as you see it and then a scene of the world as you wish it would be.

- Draw two versions of yourself: one that you think other people see when they look at you, and one that is you as you see yourself.

- Take four selfies that represent your life as it is now.

- Do an autobiography selfie series. Invite one person into your selfie who has changed your life.

Silly Shape Stories

In this activity we build a visual story together.

1. Assign students to partners.

2. Student 1 draws out several shapes on a piece of paper. They can be squiggles, lines, squares, triangles—anything you want. Get creative! Leave enough room on the paper for Student 2 to draw.

3. Student 2 uses the shapes to draw what comes to their imagination. Maybe the squiggles look like mountains. They fill in the squiggles to make them look even more like mountains. Maybe the square looks like a house; they add windows and a roof to make it look more like a house.

4. Students 1 and 2 look at what they have drawn together. They come up with a story that their drawing could tell. What figures do they have? What could those figures be doing, thinking, or feeling? Encourage students to discuss how this exercise ended up differently than they expected. Did Student 1 think that such a full story could be created through shapes? Did Student 2 expect their drawings to lead to such a full story?

You don't have to consider yourself artistic to be a visual storyteller, nor do your students. There are so many mediums now, from photography to line drawings to chalk to video to slide deck presentations. All of these are storytelling tools.

In *Brown Angels*, Walter Dean Myers gathers a series of photographs, and each accompaniment to the image is an ode to the joys, sorrows, noticings, and wonderings of a child's playful curious perspective. Images mean a lot to people in their search for story. Remember Mara, from the Introduction of this book, who carried her one and only photograph with her wherever she went. This one image inspired her daily life and her understanding of the meaning of the word *story*.

- Describe an image that tells a story you wish you could tell and write about it.
- Describe an image of a photograph you wished you had and write about it.
- Describe an image of a scene you hope to always remember and write about it.

One of our young acquaintances, at the age of 11, started an Instagram account called "ellacakery." She used cake baking and decorating as a way to express herself and tell the story of who she is. Her posts regularly received thousands of likes and comments. It was very easy for people to understand how her visual creativity was helping her tell layers of herself that would perhaps not be as easy to tell any other way. The world of story is changing before our eyes. Let us help our students empower themselves with visual and oral stories with the knowledge that they lead to writing, learning, and thinking. Let us teach them that their creations in all these forms have worth and value in the world.

3

New and Old Structures of Writing

Storytelling is about so much more than the story itself.
It is at the deepest level about who the storyteller is,
who we are as listeners, and what frame we pour our
stories into.

The structure of written text is a container for an author's thoughts and ideas. The structure and content speak to each other and, in the ideal circumstances, work together to help the student's voice be known. A confluence of content and structure help us as an audience understand what the author is trying to convey. We can help our students become effective writers, thinkers, and learners by helping them have a toolbox of these structures/containers they can use as part of how they convey ideas, perspectives, points of view, and emotion.

However, we normally have students read structured stories and then write essays about them, and a lot of those creative writing conversations are left out. If we actually want to teach students about the craft of storytelling, we need to bring into focus all of the structures, counterstructures, and rule breaks that make the construction of writing so exciting and dynamic.

We want students to know they have a voice and choices within that voice on how they want to tell their own story. We want them to know they get their own canvas, that they can be unencumbered. We need to teach structure as something that serves our story rather than something that takes over the story.

We really want them to see themselves as creative and having a lot to say. If we send a message that learning structure is another requirement you must learn before you can be elevated to a certain level of storyteller, we introduce barriers to creativity that can emerge early. Yet, structures in writing are also exciting ways to help students pour their ideas into containers that empower them or help them write with greater stamina and purpose.

In this chapter, we have identified six story structures we can use to help students take a kernel of a story and shape it. They can use these structures across content areas to help illuminate an idea they have.

1. Linear

2. Circular

3. Resistance/counterstructure

4. The hero's journey (and disrupt it!)

5. Nature-centered and event-centered

We have to frame the teaching of structures in a way that is not simply arbitrary to our students. This is what often happens with grammar. Students learn grammar as a set of rules rather than a tool that can actually help them tell better stories when in fact grammar is incredibly exciting a foundational tool for all writers. Learning structures for storytelling can fall into the same trap. You show students the three-act structure: a short first act, a really long second act where the conflict takes place, then a short third act with a resolution. When you take the structure out of the context of understanding great stories or developing your own stories, it becomes arbitrary and students are at a loss to see structure as valuable to them.

Much like teaching someone to play an instrument, teaching our students how to become competent and joyous storytellers is a combination of practice and delight. We need both. Especially for those at the beginning level of any activity, the ratio of joy to practice should be particularly high. And if the practice can be enjoyable, that is also a plus. This latter point is especially important for us to think about and put into practice when engaging with students about storytelling and writing. Many of us believe that the way to learn how to do something is to simply put our noses to the grindstone, buckle down, put in the time, power through difficulty, and keep at it with focus and intensity until we reach our goal. And at certain points in our lives, that is exactly right. The problem, though, is when we take that approach and apply it to children who are not ready for or motivated by that approach. So, this has to be fun too.

And, despite the challenges and difficulties of living in a moment in history when screens are ubiquitous and are massive distractions constantly popping up in our students' daily lives, it's important to note that technology enables all children, every single one, to be a great storyteller.

We would note that students who frequently engage as their own storytellers are going to be better able to wade through the onslaught of mainstream-generated media and stories. We live in a time when young people are inundated with information. It's on their phones, it's everywhere, and what we want a literate person to do is be able to ask questions of any text that they read. We want them to understand who the author is, who they are speaking to, where they come from, and what their biases may be. Structures help because they are a way to organize the storytelling and compose it, whether that be in a cartoon, graphic novel, memoir, or social media post.

A student who is guided by structure is like an expert tracker. Instead of feeling lost in the woods with no way out, the tracker notices the environment, such as the direction of the sun's movement. The tracker possesses security that, even in uncharted territory, they will have a plan, a technique, or an approach to get to a place they want to go to. They will have confidence and trust their ideas. They will not be afraid of the unknown and will instead be independent, bold, and fearless. This is the same feeling that a good storyteller should have going about their daily business in the world: able to analyze and think about all the stories that are presented to them as they go about their day.

Storytelling is about so much more than the story itself. It is at the deepest level about who the storyteller is, who we are as listeners, and what frame we pour our stories into. When I tell you a story, I am not simply presenting you with a chronological sequence of events that I experienced or imagined. By the stories I choose to tell and the way I choose to tell them, I am conveying information about what is important to me, what makes me happy, what makes me scared, or what makes me feel hopeful.

We can see that storytelling is much deeper than a transactional exchange in which we lay out a linear narrative for you to absorb. There are complexities and overlays and layers of depth and meaning far beyond the simple words of the narrative. And while at the youngest ages these may not be particularly nuanced or sophisticated, even (perhaps especially) the simplest stories told by our most beginning storytellers carry the deepest human connection other than the words themselves: the simple yet unimaginably profound assertion into the world, "I am here. I have something to say. I want you to hear it."

Given the almost unimaginable magnitude of what we are discussing here, what we would call the spiritual essence and meaning of storytelling is a deeply bonding human experience, and we must use every tool and technique at our disposal to engage with and help our students become storytellers and story appreciators. The good news is that, like so many things in life, these tools can be extremely and powerfully helpful when used in the right way.

Flexible frameworks create happiness. We like structure; we like routine. We also like creativity, improvisation, and the unexpected. Chaos disturbs almost all of us. Structureless situations are particularly troubling to children. The flip side is that oppressive rigidity is stifling and soul-crushing. We treasure those moments when we can come up with something new, when we do not know exactly what is coming around the corner, and when we try something different.

Flexible frameworks provide the perfect balance of structure and freedom. From a space of routine, they grow confident as writers and storytellers, able then to focus on the actual story they are telling. And with further experience and comfort, they then become comfortable exploring even more flexible frameworks, always broadening their creative options and possibilities while simultaneously operating from a place of comfort and familiarity.

Let's take a look at a variety of structures we can teach our students (in every subject area) and share that these are simply containers in which they can pour all the ideas and thoughts they have been practicing in their daily prompts.

Linear Structure

The most common structure and the easiest to recognize is linear structure: beginning, middle, and end. Linear structure's hallmarks are a sequencing of events in chronological order. Characters are introduced in the order they appear, and the narrative has a familiar and easily predictable pattern and arc. Children's fables follow such patterns, and you will see this in a child's first forays into the world of storytelling. They practice when they retell an experience as simple as "I went to the park today with Grandma, and then we came home and had lunch." Linear structure is comforting; it puts us in order. Our minds naturally process information in a linear sequence, so attempts to tell stories in a nonlinear manner require skills and craftsmanship and are a great indicator of evolution and ability as a writer. Stories meant to be told in a linear fashion that aren't (events are rearranged or characters are introduced in an unexpected order) are sometimes hard for the listener to follow, although they can provide a more vivid and intense experience for the reader/listener when well crafted.

Like a favorite sweatshirt or a beloved recipe, linear narratives appeal to us because the structure is so familiar that it is easy for us to listen to and enjoy the story. We do not have to expend brainpower trying to figure out stylistic shifts or breaks in the action that do not naturally flow one into the other.

And given that the great bulk of stories that students will have heard, even at very young ages, will be linear narratives, that framework will automatically resonate with them. The trick, then, is to help them take a storytelling structure that they have some experience with, one that makes inherent sense to them, and construct a working framework they can refer to and use to create their own linear narratives. Here we share some specific structures that relate to the narrative styles students may be hearing through read-alouds and reading independently.

The old-time seesaw of a schoolyard playground was not only a wonderful demonstration of a lever with a centered fulcrum; it was a simple way for children to entertain each other. The acronym C-SAW likewise provides a way for children to create stories to entertain each other by giving them an easy-to-use method for generating linear narratives, from the most rudimentary to the most sophisticated. Keep it simple, and even our youngest can create a good story.

Character(s)

Setting

Action

Wrap-up

Let's see how it works.

C is for character. At the most basic level, this is a jumping-off point for our most beginning writers to put a character into their story. It says something purely delightful about ourselves as human beings that we love stories so much that we are engaged as soon as we hear someone say something about a character.

"There was a girl who lived on a farm and took care of the horses."

We instinctively want to know more—immediately. What is she like? What is her life like? Where is the farm? What are the horses like? What is going to happen to her?

In fact, to make this point even more strongly, we present to you that the following is a compelling introduction to a character that will pique your interest:

"There was a girl."

That's it. That is all that is needed. With her, we have the beginnings of a story. We have laid the first stone on the path. We have begun the process of engaging the audience. It is simple, elegant, and meaningful.

This is the message we want to send to students learning to write: that simplicity, a very basic description, or a singularly unadorned character is enough to start your story. More than enough—it is all you need, and it is excellent.

By putting this affirmational feedback into the student's mind, we encourage and excite and thrill the child with the possibilities ahead. "I can do this! Already I am beginning to be a storyteller!"

There are entire styles of writing focusing on spare prose, deconstructed descriptors, plot lines so simple that they are virtually nonexistent, and endings so undramatic that saying they end with a whimper is overly generous. Meaning that "There was a girl" in some perhaps hifalutin worlds might be considered a complete story in and of itself (providing the reader with the ability to self-generate much of the other meaning). But what we will undoubtedly find with the student who begins her journey as a writer is that "There was a girl" will almost immediately lead to a strong and delightful desire to bring more depth and attributes to the character.

As with almost everything involved in teaching children, the best approach is engaged and interactive without being overly directive. Simply keep the conversation going normally. Of course, use vocabulary that the student can understand, but speak as though we are having an actual conversation and you are curious about what your student will say.

Don't be surprised or disappointed that your students may begin their first forays into writing and storytelling by mimicking other characters, stories, and styles. This is not only normal; it is absolutely crucial in helping students learn to write well. They practice story by using mentors. Students will often initially come up with characters who are exactly the same characters in games, shows, movies, or books they are familiar with: a princess, an action hero from a current video game craze, a fluffy mascot from a children's TV show, or a character from their favorite children's book. It is not a lack of creativity. It is actually a very smart strategy. We are basically asking the student to come up with a character, so they present one they know is already accepted in society and in their peer group as a legitimate character. It makes total sense! And it also provides the perfect launching pad for developing richer and unique characters of the student's own invention. Since the basic attributes of the character are already known to the student through media, right from the start they have an instant and fully functional character.

The good news is that our first goal as a teacher—to know that our student understands the concept of what a character is—has been accomplished. To build on this, teachers can engage with the student on developing their own spin on further attributes of this character. Teachers can ask students, "What is one way you can bring your character to life? How might you draw your character? What would your character's social media be like?"

Remember, when you teach someone to hit a baseball by putting it on a tee, you are doing the same thing: offering a supporting structure while the child mimics the actions and proficiency that is the ultimate goal while enabling the young learner to have the first taste of what success feels like. Modeling the characters and writing styles the student already knows is actually an incredibly powerful tool for them to use on their journey to become a writer. We will discuss this further in Chapter 5.

In addition to bringing more depth to the character, which will then make it much easier to create some interesting plot lines for the character to experience, you and the student you are working with are getting into a groove of affirmational, inquiry-based engagement. C-SAW will help the storyteller remember the key elements to a story, and it will act as a checklist for more experienced writers. Like a pilot going through a checklist before take-off on their first solo flight, making sure that everything is as it is supposed to be, or the veteran pilot going through the same checklist as a matter of routine even though they know it by heart, C-SAW grounds all writers in the deepest foundations of writing.

We look at texts differently as writers. We consume stories differently. We have lived off of certain tropes all our lives: the hero's journey and the stranger comes to town are two tropes known well in American literary canons, but there are so many more. The tropes can be reexamined. How can we diversify the structures of story? One way is to look at the many, many other ways diverse cultures tell stories and make those tropes a more natural part of our teaching and modeling.

Circular Structure

Circles are a powerful structure across many cultural traditions, evoking rituals, routines, and the ties that bind a community or environment, whether rural or urban. They honor the safety and profound resonance of that cultural group's connections to each other, to their ancestors, and to the future that keeps people together. Often, the circular structure illuminates the natural patterns of nature, of life cycles, and of time. Dorothea Susag (1998) "tells of how [Native American] spoken and written stories differ from the Western European modality of linear sequencing: "Instead of a plot characterized by rising action, climax, and falling action, [Native American] stories are frequently cyclical and episodic" (p. 43).

Stories that bring us back to the beginning are reassuring and also deeply connect to a child's internal sense of home, even if home itself is not always the easiest place to be. Students enjoy looking at text to find the ways authors bring closure by coming back to the start in the end. Use a simple circle chart to invite your students to sketch or write around the circle and tell a story they always thought of only as linear. School, after all, is a circular experience in and of itself: the student comes and goes each day. Seasons are also circular: the growth of plants and living beings followed by the leaves falling and returning. Speak to your students about these patterns and how a circle is completed. The book *Ox-Cart Man* by Donald Hall is a simple yet beautiful example of this. The farmer goes to market and sells his goods, and then he returns home each year at the same time to grow his vegetables, eventually to return once again to market. Try the following simple prompts to get students thinking in a circle:

- Write about your ideal day; start and end at the same scene.

- Write a simple opening sentence to a story, fictional or true. End the story with the same sentence with which you began.

- Make a story with visuals; have the imagery at the start and end be identical

- Think of a cycle from a subject that interests you and write a story with this cyclical process as the guiding principle. You might choose time and calendar cycles, planetary cycles, climate and weather cycles, musical cycles, geological or agricultural cycles, biological and medical cycles, or cultural and religious cycles.

Resistance/Counterstructure

Often stories are structured around a particular chronology. *This* happened, then *this* happened and then *that* happened. A structure like this can be rigid and overly scientific. Often, this involves hypotheses, data collection, and analysis. Other times, the stories follow a strict script of the hero's journey: full of expected twists and unexciting structure. Subverting this structure can forge a path of resistance and unlock novel ways of experiencing story.

Let's call out structures to show our students. The potentially most influential is how your story moves through time and space. For example, if I'm trying to tell a story in real time by calling a horse race or broadcasting a game, it's very quick; I can only get so many details. (Pam passes the ball to Ernest, and Ernest dunks and scores.) But if it's not about entertainment but about spending time, the story looks quite different: "You wouldn't believe this game we played; it was a dark and stormy night." In this case, time doesn't mean so much for you anymore. It happened a long time ago. What you're really talking about is what great friends we were and what a good and exciting time it was. Playing around with time and chronology changes our storytelling.

The power of the storyteller and whether they are societally central or displaced says a lot about these questions of chronology and time. When story is really about getting to know me, who I am, or what I believe rather than a list of happenings, there are dimensions to it that transcend and disrupt the quiet, hegemonic, masculine, and mundane structures that are in place. Think about magical realism, when seemingly crazy things can happen suddenly within the plot. At once, there's a ghost or someone disappears, or someone dies and comes back. Magical realism disrupts this straightforward, learned structure of storytelling but reflects how people experience life. It mimics how the unexpected pop up, and with this new challenge we come to understand characters with more depth.

It's not a surprise, then, that the people we've come to admire who are engaged in this kind of countercultural storytelling come from groups that are more disaffected and on the outside. Gabriel García Márquez and Toni Morrison each tell a different kind of story in a different way. It's still structured, but it's structured in a very different kind of modality. It's about getting to know people and the complexities of life.

We can see this resistance literature in early childhood texts, such as *We All Play* by Julie Flett. In this deceptively simple text, children are seen playing joyously. The animals are playfully hiding, sniffing, and sneaking. But suddenly children appear and say, "We play too! Kimetawanaw mina." The author writes, "When I was growing up, my dad shared a lot about our relationship to animals and to each other, including the land, plants, beetles, the earth, wind, water, and sky." She shares how whether we are running or watching, we are all connected, "living in relationship and care to another, in kinship." She shares with us that in Cree, this is called *wahkohtowin*. In translanguaging, Flett is centering the Cree language, the experience of connectedness. She is narrating a more inclusive structure of children's literature by not only sharing the power of this language but also centering it. It has a starring role. She also demonstrates the profound sense of well-being, parallel play, and deep joy in animals, children, and their environments. Telling new stories of joy is a form of resistance too.

In the book *Peace* by Baptiste Paul and Miranda Paul and illustrated by Esteli Meza, the authors examine the concept of peace, ostensibly for young children but really for all of us explaining the many ways peace can take different forms. There are lines that push the reader to think in new ways: "Peace is pronouncing your friend's name correctly." This is a powerful point to make, that peace is not just the absence of something but the presence of something active and intentional that might also indicate that we haven't always done a great job at these things. It challenges us to examine our own actions and take new ones. There is so much hope in this. The authors and the artist also intentionally center animals with humans in the paintings. The authors write, "The truth is that peace affects more than the humans who foster it. Peace can also impact animals and nature." They reference Mozambique, a country that was devastated by war. So many people died, and the country lost 90 percent of its wildlife. But in the time since, people have worked to restore well-being to the country. In this book about peace, the creators are resisting the simple stories we tell children about peace as a "scenario in which all human beings get along" and instead convert it to work that we must do— all of us, at all ages—to make a friend, commit to acts of kindness, and work on peace together.

In the book *What I Am* by Divya Srinivasan, the author resists the ways we generally see writing about oneself for young children. She surprises her reader with a complex and layered approach to how we introduce ourselves to others. Divha writes, "I am a daughter. I am a granddaughter. I am an Amma to my guys. I am dark. I am pale. In summer, I'm different colors. . . . I have so much. I don't have enough." The ideas are big and they are small, but they are not simple. She is challenging how we talk to children and each other about who we are and making it richer and also a little bit mysterious.

In Jason Reynolds's *Look Both Ways*, he engages in resistance narrative with a breakthrough idea for structure: he tells 10 narratives to represent the 10 blocks of a walk home. The book begins, "This story was going to begin like all the best stories, with a school bus falling from the sky." The chapters serve to illuminate the ordinary yet extraordinary lives of children, their parents, and grandparents in each of these small moments, large in the dailiness of life. In that in-between time, when children are leaving school and walking home, before they see another grown-up again, Reynolds slows down time and gives us a glimpse into the sometimes hilarious, sometimes achingly sad, stories of middle schoolers and what they really think and care about. It is about placing the stories back in their hands.

It's a book you can share with your middle school students and say, "Look, your stories are here."

In *Their Eyes Were Watching God* by Zora Neale Hurston, the narrator's voice is Janie, a Black woman in 1930s America. The resistance is the radiant, fearless life of Janie herself, told in her words, from her mind, and with her thoughts. There could have been no worse time to be a Black woman, but Hurston in every line speaks the truth of Black women's lives at that time in a way that feels as resonant today as it must have been so radical then. (It still feels radical.) She writes, "It was the time for sitting on porches," so we know we are getting ready to listen to the life of a woman. Later on, she says of Janie, "She saw her life like a great tree in leaf with things that suffered, things enjoyed, things done and undone." The book is written in the dialect of Black southern folks, talking in their most authentic voices, the dialogue itself reflecting resistance to the patriarchy, to racism by saying this of Janie: she has a voice, it is a singular voice, it is her voice, and it is her story.

These books can serve as models for us to share with our students, to show them what resistance stories can look like. Resistance doesn't have to mean that we turn away from love; our resistance can be in the context of love and leaning toward what we care about and what we all find kindred. Resistance is about saying something brave and big, about telling stories in new ways and in voices that urgently must be heard and shared, and about using powerful and intentional about using craft elements to say, "I am here. My story matters. And I am here to tell it."

Let's help our students see the potential of resistance stories and narratives to reframe their own lives and speak their authentic selves.

- Write a story in which the quietest character talks the most.
- Write a true story, but incorporate an unexpected imaginary event to reveal a big theme or idea you carry with you.

- Write a story where each chapter, section, paragraph, or line is told from a different character's perspective.

- Write a story that disrupts the hierarchies you notice in society. Give voice to characters in your life or imagination who you want to make loud and strong.

- Write a story of active resistance: find a rule, law, or community practice you find unjust and try to write your way to a solution. This could be as big a picture as civil rights or as specific as your school's dress code. Use a personal or family story to bring this action to life.

The Hero's Journey (and Disrupt It!)

One of the most familiar of the narrative forms is what we call the hero's journey. We see it of course in *The Odyssey* and *Lord of the Rings*, *Harry Potter*, and *Star Wars*. These tales maintain a very strict structure: the hero (generally male and white) leaves home and travels far away, solving a problem or facing a challenge or going on a quest, before returning home triumphant. The author P. L. Travers, who wrote *Mary Poppins*, actually may have been subverting this very structure with her own story of a stern, uncompromising single woman, childless (shocking!) who comes to the Banks' home and changes them forever. Her point of view was this:

> Could it be . . . that the hero is one who is willing to set out, take the first step, shoulder something? Perhaps the hero is one who puts his foot upon a path not knowing what he may expect from life but in some way feeling in his bones that life expects something of him (Travers, 1976).

Authors Hartmut Koenitz, Andrea Di Pastena, Dennis Jansen, Brian de Lint, and Amanda Moss (2018) argue that there is more to story than the hero's journey: exposition, rising tension/conflict followed by a climactic event that serves to de-escalate the central conflict, and a conclusion that often involves a return to the "normal state of affairs." While this Western understanding is the most persuasive, they cite many other types of story structure that disrupt it, including "Kishōtenketsu, a conflict-free narrative structure originating in Chinese poetry and widely used in Korean and Japanese writing; the Robleto, a Nicaraguan narrative structure defined by a notable line of repetition; and frame narrative structures from the Indo-Arab literary and oral traditions (p. 5); and others.

If our students would like to tell a story that follows the hero's journey, this is a great exercise in writing. However, writing instruction should never end there. Let us empower our students to practice centering stories of people who have been silenced or historically marginalized. Stories give us strength and hope to be writers in a world where no one's voice is missing. We can ask

- What does it mean to be a hero?
- How do you envision a hero, and what does this say about your preconceptions?
- How could we rewrite the expected narrative so that the hero is unlikely and so that the journey feels new and different?
- What can we do to be the hero of our own stories?
- Think about someone in your family who is important to you. How would you write a hero's journey story that features or centers them?

Nature-Centered and Event-Centered

Give young people the opportunity to see narrative structure as not always centered on people alone. They can also learn to write vividly and expressively about landscape, living things, and layered textures of everyday life.

Navajo culture teaches that "water was given to us, and it has specific prayers and a specific name and water has a song. There are specific songs that are just water songs. There's a way of speaking to water and greeting water and making a relationship with water, the same way you make a relationship with your mother" (Shapiro, 2021).

Mallory Whiteduck (2013) discusses how Màmiwininiwag or Algonquin people often tell oral histories in relationship to the land: "Our stories represent a fundamental love and respect for our home-land" (p. 72). Craig Howe elaborates in the same article, "Rather than being linear, these stories are event centered: here something happened and a particular person or being was present. . . . Often, as the storyteller is reciting an account of an event, another trigger is tripped and another narrative begins" (p. 79).

Event-centered storytelling often incorporates setting centrally. Many in the Deaf community in the United States use American Sign Language (there are many other dialects of sign language in different countries, but here we are focusing on ASL). The storytelling in the Deaf community is event-centered. For example, if you are telling a story in ASL, you will set the story up in space—showing where everyone is with hand motions, sometimes pointing to where the action is going to happen, and then moving people and objects around you as you sign the story.

- Write a story from the point of view of a tree, water, a fallen leaf, or a star.

- Write a story of gratitude about the ways nature helps you, your community, or your culture.

- Write a story that centers around a specific event. Before you write about characters, describe in detail the space of the story.

● ● ●

When we teach students about the craft of storytelling, we bring all of these different structures and rule breaks into play.

It is a true wonder how we are programmed to tell stories and have stories told to us. Expectations that seem to be hardwired into us, and then developed from the first moments we first hear the words of others spoken around us, inform what we anticipate in a story. There will be characters. There will be a setting, someplace (imaginary or real) where something happens to the character, physical or emotional, or both (the action). We love a story that has some tension, some question about whether an outcome we might hope for comes to pass. We love a twist or surprise, something perhaps unanticipated but exciting. And we still in our deepest hearts hope for a happy ending, a satisfying conclusion, a wrap-up that makes logical and emotional sense.

We can see that storytelling is much, much deeper than a transactional exchange in which someone lays out a linear narrative for an audience to absorb it. There are complexities and overlays and layers of depth and meaning far beyond the simple words of the narrative. And while at the youngest ages these may not be particularly nuanced or sophisticated, even (perhaps especially) the simplest stories told by our most beginning storytellers carry the deepest human connection other than the words themselves. They are a simple yet unimaginably profound assertion into the world: "I am here. I have something to say. I want you to hear it." And when the listener responds to that story, no matter how short, no matter how simple, no matter how silly, no matter how nonsensical it may be, there is a human connection that is like a bolt of lightning between two independent souls, signaling in the deepest recesses of the child's heart that this world is good, for there is another being who sees them and wants to know what they have to say. The simplicity of Margaret Wise Brown's *Goodnight Moon* is deceptive. She is helping the youngest child understand that traveling into the darkness of sleep is a journey in and of itself, layered with complexity, anxiety, and comfort. With these examples, we can show even the youngest writers how narrative ignites thought, carries us through difficult journeys, and makes sense of a confusing world.

Let's instill in every student an irreversible self-conception of someone who can write and therefore can be a storyteller, tell their story to the world, and have that spark of connection with another human being. This is very serious territory we are venturing into here, which is why it is essential to share with them a toolbox for a diversity of structures that will fit the ideas they want to share and expand.

Our students can tell stories the world can hear and understand if they have the structures to help them. For those who have great difficulty writing, it is a life-changing gift you can give them: to show them the structures that will be toolkits for how they can place their stories at the center of experience and life and community. For those who are comfortable with writing, this is an added benefit to open new and varied ways of telling their stories.

We can teach our students that narrative structures too can provide us great freedom to express love and ourselves, and we must not forget that the structures we offer must be diverse and wide-ranging so everyone's voice can be heard.

4

Using Mentor Texts

Exemplars and role models are a gateway to growing confident writers.

This chapter focuses on the reading our students take in. When students read, they breathe in written language—words, grammar, structures, and form—so they can breathe out their best writing. Storytelling is what lives between each breath.

The books we select for our mentor writing work should show the diversity, beauty, and complexity of the human experience—past and present—and the languages, perspectives, joys, and dreams writers express through a wide variety of genres and styles. They should show the extraordinary empathy great writers have: their capacity to inhabit the lives of their characters (and self-empathy as in the case of memoir).

Writing stories gives us the ultimate power to shape the narrative of the story we are writing and also the life we are living. We emulate the narratives of the world of writers and take in their voices and their styles and ways of shaping through structure, grammar, punctuation, and more, and these techniques and craft elements become part of our own voices and styles too. Only it's not just "copying," it's drinking in the magnificence of our mentors and letting their inspiration guide us to our own voice.

We can help students of all ages walk through the ways a specific writer builds a world for and with us. Teaching writing is about following in the footsteps of the great ones and the newly discovered ones, putting your foot down into the imprint of what is already there, testing your own foot to the size, and then, when ready, stepping off into a new path of your own.

Our students have to become close readers of text if they are to become the author of their own ideas. Let's show our students all the possibilities in the world of writing so they are able to both see all that is possible and be inspired to do what has never been done.

Part of getting students to see themselves as the authors they look up to is to simply ask them to create in the genres they consume. Sometimes books are just the right source to find test answers. If students have other types of storytelling to look to as a source of guidance, they will more easily see them as their role models. If you are going to design a video game, you'll look to great video game makers and designers. If you are going to be a hip-hop artist and you want to be better than Jay-Z, you memorize all the lyrics and the way he presents his work to the public. If you are going to be a poet, you might look to Walt Whitman, Emily Dickinson, or Langston Hughes to see how they handle line breaks, metaphor, and rhythm.

Part of it is just in the ask. If a student likes a graphic novel, ask them to write one. Ask a student to write a verse that follows the same structure as their favorite rap song. Ask a student to write about a gymnast they admire and their last floor routine. If you are asking them to write a picture book, ask them to bring in or select favorite picture books and what they like about them. When we immerse our students in these forms and types, they begin producing in those same genres or modalities. The ones our students naturally feel passionate about give them energy to really emulate other pros, much in the way athletes do when they watch hours and hours of their favorite heroes on the field. One is passing their inspiration and skill onward to the next. The same is true in writing, and we can set up our classrooms to reflect that spirit.

Let's feature authors across disciplines and grade levels and let them speak to us. We can use their inspiration and wisdom to give students and our community ways to write and to grow as writers. In this chapter, we share authors who are changing lives through their approach to storytelling and who use story structures and narrative art forms to push us toward story embedded in and leveraged by masterful craft. In this chapter, we will share techniques authors use with specific examples and how students can try them in their own writing.

In our exercises we ask, "How can students be strategic with literacy devices to achieve deeper goals? How can student writers use exemplary authors to convince their readers of something, move an audience to tears, or teach us a lesson?" With these exercises, we can focus on the deeper ways authors are brilliantly using craft to convey emotion, time, rhythm, and impact. What is compelling them, moving them, and driving them? What was in this author that needed to get out so urgently that it became this story we are all reading here today? With exercises that draw attention to core understanding, we are reminding our students that the grammar and spelling rules we learn in the classroom are a toolkit toward conveying the message we want to get across. Truly great writing comes from the deepest place of who we are and who we want to be, and *grammatical, structural tools are the ship upon which we sail our best ideas.*

Here we share seven wonderful books to share a system of teaching writing that can then be transferred to virtually any book you and your students love. Reading an excellent children's book is an exciting way to bring you and your students of all ages inside the mind of a brilliant craftsperson.

For each book, we identified book themes and features, craft elements, information about the author with a warm-up, some writing prompts to try, and connection to the power of story.

Book 1: *Knuffle Bunny* by Mo Willems (kindergarten)

Noteworthy Book Features:

- Humor
- Character expression
- Dialogue
- Mixed media: photography and illustrations
- Lost toys

A Look at Mo Willems and What He Does Best

Mo Willems uses humor, dialogue, and character expression to tell us so much about this story's characters' emotional fluctuations. Ask your K–1 classrooms about illustrations and humor as a warm-up.

- What's your favorite illustration in this book? What do you love about it? Why do some books have pictures?
- Talk with a partner about a family story or memory that makes you laugh.

Craft Elements

Humor: What makes you laugh? What page really made you smile? Turn and talk with a partner about what Mo did with his writing and drawing that got you smiling.

Character expressions: What do you think Trixie is feeling at the beginning, middle, and end of the story? What shows this in her expressions? With the class, chart out in pictures how they think Trixie is feeling at the beginning, middle, and end, using illustrations if you like. How do you know how she is feeling? Now, try this same exercise for her father.

Dialogue: Why does Trixie say, "Aggle flaggle klabble"? Why can't her father understand her?

Try It

- Ask your classroom to create two characters, imaginary or real. Create a setting that is a lot like where you live, and be as specific as you can. Where is this scene? Is it a street corner? Is it on the subway? On a dirt road? Now have your characters talk to one another!

- Discuss punctuation marks, like exclamation points, with your classroom. How can punctuation describe emotion and mood? Ask young learners how they can use punctuation to make their characters speak with lively personality.

- Ask young learners to try writing a story that includes only or mostly all dialogue! How can dialogue tell your story?

- Draw a picture of yourself, a family member, or a favorite character. Make the character happy. Draw another picture with that same character but show them feeling sad. Now try other emotions!

The Power of This Story

Recently, we were working with a 1st-grade class and studying Mo Willems's book *Knuffle Bunny*. His fine and delightful art introduced us to a world of whimsical care and empathy. In this book the father has just realized he has left the child's bunny at the laundromat. He runs comically through the street to retrieve the precious stuffed animal. Later, as we work alongside one of our student writers, she says, "I am going to draw like Mo Willems today. I am going to show surprise with my character's eyebrows going way up just like Mo did in his writing." Already at such a young age the child writer is well aware of craft elements, such as the emphasis that artist is placing on aspects of the character's emotional response to the happenings of the story. They are aware of the connection between emotions of each character and the dialogue happening between them. Not to mention, they recognize some of the humor interconnected with those things too.

Book 2: *Fry Bread* by Kevin Noble Maillard (1st–2nd grades)

Noteworthy Book Features:

- Food
- Metaphor
- Repetition
- Culture and heritage
- Tradition

A Look at Kevin Noble Maillard and What He Does Best

Kevin Noble Maillard is a law professor and journalist interested in illuminating "hidden" stories. "Of course," Kevin notes, "these stories are in plain sight, and now we have more writers influencing the flow of attention to these narratives." As a warm-up, ask your young learners the following:

- What's a food that is precious to you or your family?
- Think of a family tradition that is in "plain sight" to you but that your friends or teachers might not know about. Explain it to a partner.

Craft Elements

Ask about food and culture: Why do you think fry bread is so important to the characters of this story? Why and how might food be a powerful tool for storytelling?

Discuss repetitive refrain: Kevin repeats, "Fry bread is _____," inserting *shape, sound, color, flavor, time, art, history, place, nation, everything, us,* and *you.* Why?

Teach metaphor: How can a food be place? How can a food be time? What does Kevin Maillard mean when he says this? Discuss metaphors.

Try It

- Ask students about their culture and heritage. What's an "artifact" of your family? Think of something important to you and your family, your culture, your traditions, and more. For one, it might be their grandfather's zaatar bread because it represents their Lebanese heritage, or perhaps it's a giant three-legged race one plays with their family every summer. Maybe it is a painting on your wall, an old watch, or a sacred story. Brainstorm what this artifact represents. What does it say about who you are? Why is it important?

  » Write, "[Artifact] is _____" (sharing, community, nourishment, fun, family, laughter) with each one on a separate page of a story. Then accompany each with a drawing.

  » Use the refrain as Kevin Maillard does—"Fry bread is sound . . . fry bread is color"—but use your own food as a metaphor to try this refrain and see what effect it has on your writing. See if you can add other metaphors to your writing.

- Ask your students about storytelling and community. What's a story of your family's? Think of a story that your mother, father, grandparent, or sibling often tells or one everyone in your immediate or extended family would remember. Then, tell it from the perspective of each of the people who are in it. Why is it meaningful to each person individually?

The Power of This Story

The importance of books like *Fry Bread* cannot be understated. Not only does this book introduce metaphor and the ways they can create a beautiful and moving texture to a story, *Fry Bread* also invites young readers and writers to explore their own culture and family's traditions within the context of the classroom. Asking about this reiterates to our young learners that their family, culture, heritage, food, and traditions are story worthy. Asking students to tell these stories within the classrooms situates them as important enough to be written, shared with their classmates, and even published someday. It reminds them they have the talent to be world-changing readers and writers with the eloquence, knowledge, and skills to tell it better than anyone.

Book 3: *Bright Star* by Yuyi Morales (2nd–4th grades)

Noteworthy Book Features:

- Translanguaging
- Using 2nd person and the word *you*
- Varying perspectives
- Repetition
- Imagery
- Animals
- Color and texture

A Look at Yuyi Morales and What She Does Best

Yuyi Morales, a Mexican American author and illustrator of children's picture books, uses repetition, the Spanish language, and beautiful illustrations to share this unique and heartwarming story. Yuyi is known for drawing inspiration from stories of her family and her heritage for her books. Yuyi loves using color and textures "as another way to reveal the heart of the story." Invite your students to warm up with the following prompts:

- What's your favorite animal and why? Draw a picture of this creature and write a three-sentence story about it.
- Think of a family memory that brings up feelings of contentment and joy. Then, using art materials, words, collage, technology, or any other modality, show the textures and colors this memory evokes.

Craft Elements

Ask about repetition: Why do you think Yuyi kept repeating, "You are a bright star inside our hearts"? How did it make you feel? How can you use repetition when you write to someone's emotions?

Discuss the importance of language: This author uses Spanish to convey powerful emotion. Ask your students how they might translanguage in a story they are writing to convey the multitude of culture language. (Even the youngest children can do this.)

Prompt conversation about illustrations and images: Notice the patterns, choices of color, and moods Yuyi conveys. How can you do this in your writing and drawing?

Try It

- Draw a picture of your favorite animal. Now pretend that animal is you! What would you say to yourself? Use a "You are . . ." phrase.

- Write a story that uses repetition. Write a story that has the same phrase repeated on every page. What will you choose to repeat throughout your story? Why that phrase? How will you craft a story around it?

- Yuyi tells a story from a fawn's point of view. Can you do the same with an animal of your choice? What animal conveys the emotion you want to share?

- Yuyi's fawn ventures out into the world with a gentle voice to guide and support her. Are there words someone has said to you to give you courage? Write them down, and use them to tell a longer story.

The Power of This Story

With lyrical writing and beautiful illustrations, Yuyi Morales uses both Spanish and English to show us a powerful way of writing that journeys between both. Not only does this validate translanguaging within our students' learning as a completely acceptable writing practice, but it also shows everyone in the classroom how beautiful this practice is. Moreover, *Bright Star* centers language as a starring role in the story and in the characters' experiences.

Book 4: *Front Desk* by Kelly Yang (4th–6th grades)

Noteworthy Book Features:

- Cultural identity
- Immigration and newcomers
- Character development
- Narrative power
- Self-growth
- Belonging

A Look at Kelly Yang and What She Does Best

Author Kelly Yang immigrated from China with her family at the age of 6, first learning English when she arrived. By age 13, Kelly went to college, and by 17 continued on to law school before ultimately deciding to pursue her passion for writing. Kelly's character development reminds us of the importance of a sense of belonging. Ask middle grades the following questions as a warm-up:

- Similar to the character of Mia, Kelly herself was once a young newcomer in the United States learning a new language. Have you been a newcomer anywhere, not necessarily from another country, but new to a community? Can you share that experience?

- What does it mean to belong? When is a time you had to enter a new community, and what made you feel most welcomed?

Craft Elements

Discuss character development: How does Mia change throughout this story? Draw or write about how she has changed with a time line. Put a star next where she made a big leap forward. Do the same for your own life. Make a self-portrait time line, and note your big changes.

Discuss narrative and themes: At the motel, Mia develops an understanding of and truths about racism, bigotry, poverty, and unfairness. How do these discoveries affect Mia along her journey? How does author Kelly Yang weave these discoveries into the narrative? How do you envision including a social justice theme in your writing?

Compare and contrast: Select two different letters from this book and compare and contrast them. What do these two letters tell us about the book's themes? What do they tell us about Mia's growth? Use this technique in your writing.

Try It

- Select a character from a story you've written in the past or one you hope to write in the future. Then write out this character's backstory. What happened before we're introduced to this character? What is this character's favorite colors, foods, or genres of music? What is their family like? What is their most precious childhood memory? Think about how these new discoveries about your character will help you more effectively tell your story.

- Letters can have a big impact in life, and now we see how they can affect a story too. Try writing a letter to someone in your life you have difficulty talking with or to someone you'd like to express love or appreciation for.

- Write a short story that a younger version of you would have loved to read at a challenging time in your life. Maybe this short story explores something you were experiencing at the time but didn't have the language to describe. Maybe this story features a character you would have related to, learned from, or looked up to.

The Power of This Story

Organic, natural storytelling happens when a story celebrates characters and stories that are accessible, relatable, and authentic. This story shows flawed characters growing, making mistakes, and growing again and deals with themes pertaining to real experiences— good and bad. It's imperative that our learners see their life reflected back to them, with young people who look like them or have a similar hobby or fear. When kids are excited by these stories, they start to write better. Stories like *Front Desk* expand the horizons of those who are not close to Mia's experiences, and they affirm the power of their own local narratives to those who are. Kelly Yang's rich character development exemplifies powerful lessons in belonging.

Book 5: *El Deafo* by Cece Bell (6th grade)

Noteworthy Book Features:

- Friendship
- Overcoming hardships
- Community
- Belonging
- Difference
- Graphic novels and illustrations
- Imagination

A Look at Cece Bell and What She Does Best

Author and illustrator Cece Bell uses a mixture of imagination and illustrations to tell a complex story of the joys and hardships that can come with being different from others. Ask students to warm up with the following questions:

- Who is your favorite superhero? What powers do they have? What weaknesses do they have? Are those powers and weaknesses related?
- Have you ever felt different from others? What was it that made you feel different from your friends or family? Talk about it.

Craft Elements

Discuss the benefits of a little imagination: Cece uses her imagination to make herself into a superhero. She imagines herself to be a hero and fights the villains and obstacles in her life. Her imagination allows her to express how she really feels about people and situations. Sometimes when she's not paying attention, Cece's imagination becomes reality, and she says and does things she only imagined herself to do. When has your imagination escaped into reality? Can imagination change reality? How can imagination empower us to act differently and change our lives?

Notice the illustrations: Look at the ways in which Cece's imagination is illustrated. The illustrations give us perspective into Cece's mind and the profound way in which Cece sees the world. How can illustrations help us see things from a different point of view? Do the illustrations help us better understand Cece and how she feels in certain situations? What can we learn from illustrations that we can't learn from the words alone?

Prompt about graphic novels: Cece's story is told in the form of a graphic novel. With a graphic novel we can see what the characters are saying, thinking, and feeling by reading speech bubbles, observing their expressions, and witnessing characters interact with one another. Pick a page from *El Deafo* and look at the ways in which the words and illustrations work together to help us understand the story. What do the illustrations tell us that the words don't? When do we need the words to understand what is happening? How would the story be different if we had no illustrations? How do we convey our deepest emotions through multimedia?

Try It

- What superpowers do you have? (If you can't think of one, think of one you would want.) How do these superpowers help you overcome your daily struggles and hardships? Write about yourself and a superpower you naturally have.

- Center visual storytelling. This can look like writing a graphic novel, illustrating a picture book, or even creating a visual storyboard for organizing a longer story you'd like to write. You could also try choosing a character from a previously written story or story idea and drawing them with their families and friends. If you don't consider yourself an artistic person, don't sweat it! These visuals don't have to be for anyone else's eyes but your own if that makes you feel more comfortable. Don't worry about perfection; focus on the joy in exploring your story's world visually. See what centering visual storytelling changes about your written work.

- Draw yourself as a superhero.

The Power of This Story

Graphic novels can be a great starting point for older students with reading and writing anxiety, as it centers visual storytelling, a modality that is often more familiar and comfortable for many. For students who struggle with the many rules of standard English conventions, suggesting they write a story as a graphic novel can make the task feel more manageable and fun while continuing to help these students hone their writing skills. Rather than staring at an ominous blank page, these students can begin by imagining their story idea visually and add in writing as it services the pictures. *El Deafo* can help students who feel vulnerable about their writing skills see the many valid and celebrated visual forms published writing can take and help empower them to try it in their own writing. Cece Bell also reminds us of the power of vulnerability in *El Deafo*, as the character Cece grows to understand her difference as her superpower. A story like *El Deafo* reminds kids, at a pivotal moment in their social development, that they belong within their community no matter how different they may feel and this very difference makes them world changers.

Book 6: *Look Both Ways* by Jason Reynolds

Noteworthy Book Features:

- Empathy
- Humor and sorrow combined

- 3rd-person perspective
- Setting and details
- Friendship
- Interwoven narrative

A Look at Jason Reynolds and What He Does Best

Jason Reynolds uses humor, sorrow, 3rd-person point of view, and dialogue to tell 10 stories. Ask students the following warm-up questions:

- Talk with a partner about what you do after school. Do you have any activities or things you look forward to? What's the journey home like?
- Who is someone you want to travel with or feel comfortable journeying with?

Craft Elements

Discuss humor: These stories are funny, but they are also serious. Look closely at how Jason Reynolds does this by looking at one small part that seems funny but also real.

Note 3rd-person point of view: This gives Jason Reynolds the chance to tell multiple stories. He puts you in the minds of different characters. Third-person perspective is powerful because it allows the author to give you the big picture of what's happening and in multiple perspectives. Consider a story you are writing or telling. Could you tell your own story from a 3rd-person perspective?

Ask about dialogue: How does the dialogue in the stories captivate you? What is a standout conversation?

Try It

- Take a few minutes to think about what you do when you are going to school or coming home. Write a short story in

3rd-person point of view about your best memory. Who was with you? What were you talking about? Why do you think it feels important to you?

- Draw a group of characters and add speech bubbles to your drawing. Reynolds uses realistic dialogue to tell the stories of his characters. What dialogue will you use?

- How does setting influence story? Write the same story in two different settings. What do you notice about your two versions? What do you notice about your characters? Use the kinds of specific details that Reynolds does.

The Power of This Story

Pro-empathy means we are in active work around how we can inhabit the worlds of others and how we can take tender care of ourselves. Literacy and the power of story show us how to empathetically perspective-take. Every book and every story we read is an author attempting to make the world stronger by writing their way into an understanding of the human spirit and the human condition. Empathy is an analysis we are consistently working on as we read. *Look Both Ways* not only subverts typical narrative structures, resisting by offering multiple chapters in different perspectives and playing with the concept of time, but it also invites every student to practice empathy.

Book 7: *You Should See Me in a Crown* by Leah Johnson (high school)

Noteworthy Book Features:

- Family
- Friendship
- Identity

- Overcoming hardships
- Technology
- Romance
- High school

A Look at Leah Johnson and What She Does Best

Leah Johnson is an award-winning author of books for children and young adults who uses dialogue, 1st-person point of view, and conflict to tell the story of Liz Lighty and the challenges she faces to achieve her goals. Ask students to warm up with the following questions before reading:

- Talk with a partner about what you do outside of school. Are there any clubs, sports, or extracurricular activities that you participate in? If not, are there any you would like to participate in?
- How would you define friendship?

Craft Elements

Discuss dialogue: What do you think about the dialogue in the stories and how the characters talk to each other? What do you think it adds to the story? Look back through a chapter that stands out to you and only read the dialogue. Then share your observations with a partner.

Ask about 1st-person point of view: Why do you think it's important that the book was told through Liz's 1st-person point of view? What do you think we gain from this point of view? Make a list and share with a partner.

Ask about narrative conflict: Liz overcomes challenges and hardships in the story surrounding her identity, friendships, and personal goals. Can you connect to one of these conflicts from a narrative in your own life? How might you tell that story?

Try It

- Using 1st-person point of view, tell a short story about any day you've experienced in the past two weeks. Include your thoughts and what you saw, heard, or felt. Feel free to include text messages like Leah Johnson does for Liz's story.

- Create a comic strip that is solely based on dialogue with minimal narration. Who are your characters? What are they talking about? What do you learn about them from their conversation?

- Think about a conflict you've had recently. Create a conflict resolution map. This can be portrayed in any way (feel free to use your imagination). Just answer the following questions in the map: What was the main conflict? Why did this conflict occur? How did you feel when you had this conflict and why? How did you resolve the conflict? Did anyone help you? How did you feel after the conflict was resolved?

- Create a self-awareness map with your name in the middle and bubbles around it. Pretend each bubble represents a part of your identity, and fill in the bubbles with what words you would use to describe yourself. Share a new way of seeing yourself with a partner. Use the map to write a new narrative.

The Power of This Story

Giving students a book like *You Should See Me in a Crown*, which delves into the complex world of high school relationships while tackling larger themes like identity, helps high school students see their own lives, anxieties, and friendships reflected back to them. The book's use of technology, including text messages throughout, helps de-hierarchize different types of writing and demonstrate to students that their writing—even their quick messages to friends—can play a role in great storytelling. Getting students to see themselves as the authors they look up to is to ask them to create in the genres they consume. *You Should See Me in a Crown* reminds students of the many ways they are already working with story. If students have many types of storytelling to look to as a source of guidance, they will begin to see themselves as their writing role models and further harness the power of story.

How to Craft a Power of Story Mentor Lesson

While these stories and prompts encourage our learners to emulate craft elements of some incredible children's and young adult authors, these activities are only a small fraction of the possibilities in lesson planning around mentor texts and authors. The most important aspect of deciding how to craft a lesson around the power of story is to select books for our classroom that exemplify diversity and a variety of perspectives. This includes picking books that speak to your classroom's interests and hobbies. It means giving students access to books in their language, with characters that look and feel like them. It means exposing them to books with a wide variety of genre and style in a variety of reading levels.

Writing stories gives us the ultimate power to shape not only our writing but also our lives. Students will begin to emulate the narratives of the text-rich community of belonging we create. When formulating prompts and talking points around each text, return to our principles for a community of belonging.

Center joy. Think of the activities that would be joyful specifically for your students. How can these moments of joy fit into your writing instruction lesson? Don't shy away from making these prompts fun!

Be a deep listener. Listen deeply to what your students enjoy within the classroom as well as outside the classroom. What are they into right now? How do they spend their time? What classroom activities are they always asking to fit into the day? Incorporate their interests into writing lessons by choosing books that speak to your learners and prompting them to discuss their passions within their work.

Value wonder. Make time for asking questions about others' writing. This can be mentor authors and classroom peers. Invite students to go into any reading experience with the understanding that every decision by the author was carefully and intentionally included. Prompt students to wonder why the author did what they did.

Prioritize creativity and value student innovation. Allow students to respond to mentor texts in new and innovative ways. Perhaps a student wants to make a song inspired by a story or paint a canvas. Let students create in the modality they feel comfortable, and then ask them to write with their creations as their muse.

Become problem solvers. While we are most interested in writing and storytelling skills, it is important to ask craft element and reading comprehension questions as well. This prompting helps get students interested in narrative structures, characterization, and other toolkit techniques to create their own story. Ask students to problem solve specific moments in the texts with questions about how characters were feeling or why a character made a certain decision.

Make pro-empathy a core value. Include books that students can relate to but also some that they cannot. It is important that students have both mirrors and windows in the stories around them. Give them books that offer a glimpse into someone else's reality and life experience so they are able to practice perspective taking and empathy. Give them books that represent them to help them practice self-love.

Create story and writing routines. While you craft lessons, follow a relatively similar structure so students learn what to expect. For example, start with a warm-up activity and end with a try-it exercise!

Help students thrive independently. While collaborative storytelling can yield incredible work and community, give students moments to work on these skills independently.

Interrupt negative thinking and turn to the positive. We don't want mentor text lessons to turn into harmful comparisons between author and student. Remind learners that wherever they are in their storytelling skills journey is OK, and remember to praise their work often for its strengths.

Celebrate every day. Celebrate the work students do as a result of author and text studies by having a celebratory share-out class, or offer prizes or stickers to students for their incredible work!

We can help students of all ages discover and explore the way writers build a world for and with us. As we teach writing, we help our students follow in the footsteps of great authors while inviting them to creatively and innovatively forge their own path.

Power of Story Lesson Checklist

- Centers joy
- Includes the specific interests of the classroom
- Values wonder
- Prioritizes creativity and values student innovation
- Keeps kids problem solving with craft element questions
- Is pro-empathy
- Has a fixed structure
- Includes independent time
- Interrupts negative thinking and turns to the positive
- Is celebratory

5

Conferring and Assessment

Assessment should be multifaceted, collaborative,
and nonjudgmental.

Let's engage in practical ways to confer with students that honor how they are discovering themselves and literacy all at the same time. For an assessment plan that feels vivid, emotional, connected, authentic, and structured, writer evaluations should be multifaceted, collaborative, and nonjudgmental.

"We measure what we treasure." In schools, we sometimes as a system really don't. We talk about valuing student voices and helping them say what they mean and learn how to tell and write stories clearly and with purpose. And yet, our measurements are often the direct opposite of this. We tend to zero in right away on the technical parts of story: sentence structure, grammar, and format. But there needs to be a better way to identify what we really want from a piece of writing and know how we can help students become stronger writers and storytellers by giving the kind of feedback that can really work.

What does it mean to help create the space where this kind of genius is unpacked? We must find a balance between one end of the spectrum, where there is complete teacher-focused instruction, and the other, where everyone's first try is brilliant and there are no pedagogies that make students feel inferior. Let's understand that students have stories inside them, but it's hard work to help pull them out. That is a very important part of your work. It's hard work to help students develop the self-reflection needed to improve their skills. There's a very specific role that we have to play, and it's important. Students have stories, but they need cultivation, a pedagogy, and someone to walk with them to bring them out.

Doing this well is a part of what will define powerful teaching in the mid-21st century: How do teachers play a role that facilitates creativity? It's challenging. You don't want to simply say, "Well, that whole scene is wrong; redo it." But you do want to ask some questions such as, "What did you hear that was missing? Share some other examples of how others have done it," and become a dynamic interlocutor with the student trying to create something. Our students are naturally storytellers, but we can help add life to those stories and give them techniques to be able to share those stories.

Cultivating story is a phrase we can use with our students. They come with ideas that are not perfectly baked yet, but this is actually the perfect scenario for quality education. If you think the person that you're engaging with is wholly dependent upon your knowledge, it becomes very one-sided. But the pendulum swings the other way too. We can think about what students bring to the classroom that helps make them better versions of the selves they want to be. This happens when you think about the storytelling instruction we want. There's a role for teachers to play, and students bring so much to us.

Measure authenticity by asking questions like

- How often are children able to tell their own stories?

- Was a student interrupted?

- Did they get to speak in the classroom, and was it of their own volition?
- Was there a natural audience for it?
- In what domain did this storytelling occur? Spoken? Written? Drawn? Acted out? Digital modality?

We can measure quality by asking questions like "What would it mean for someone to become a better storyteller than they were, or what would it mean to improve the kind of quality of storytelling overall?" Authenticity and voice help us answer some of these. A student's use of language and the fluency with which they were able to tell their own stories can help organize this measure.

It's also important to understand the particular genres of storytelling. As writers, our students can use all the different modalities of storytelling to inform their writing style and success as writers. For example, we can practice tone or pace as speakers and then apply that practice to our writing. If I'm telling a story through acting, it could be body and performance, and then when I move back to my writing, I have a much more holistic connection to lived emotion that can be applied to that piece. If it is a story that I'm drawing, I can play with mood, tone, and purpose and then apply those dimensions to my writing itself. When students can practice their stories in multiple modalities, they can experience their own stories more fully and bring that extra depth of understanding to their writing.

In writing conferences with students, we must prioritize student voice rather than top-down judgment on their storytelling work. In a conversation in a writing conference with a student, you can ask, "What did you notice? What did you hear? Will you read it out loud to me?" When they say something like, "I didn't say enough about my grandma," that is when we know they are able to hear their voice and have a dialogue about it.

From a very young age, we want students to be able to put their eyes on their own work and have a conversation about it. "What did *you* think? What did you like? Where did you get stuck? How can I, your teacher, help you remove the obstacles to get the result you want?"

Conferring is really all about hearing our students talk out loud, whether beside us in person or online, about where they are at in their process. With this framework, the student will eventually be able to say, "I really like this character, and I think I see some places where we might give him more voice." The student might notice, "My piece starts out really strong and ends really strong, but it's the middle where we get lost. How do I get my characters from the ice cream shop to the forest in a more dynamic way?" *Powerful assessment is really a dialogue where students get to take ownership.*

We want the writing process to be collaborative and iterative and ongoing. One of the worst things that we can have is a grading system that feels like a bad birthday present: you open up the assignment at the end, and you're totally shocked at what's inside of it. We know so much more now that we really should have a lot of affirmation at the end. That starts at the beginning. We need to ask the questions that allow us to understand what the student wants to accomplish in the assignment. You are often the first and most important audience of their work.

In one conference we looked at the first draft, and the student wanted to add much more detail. We asked, "How do you feel about it now?" and the student learned how to respond in their own words: "You know, I feel much better, but I have some questions here." We want to activate student thinking and student voice in their self-analysis. The key is to unlock two things: the student's own unique voice and the student's ability to become a co-assessor of their own work. This is true for our youngest students too. We can position them with something like, "Hey, I wonder if you can listen for this and tell me what you hear."

We don't want to be didactic. We don't want to make presumptions. We want students to really be the leaders of the conference after a while. This may not be the case at the beginning of the school year—certainly not in the first assignment—but it should happen as soon as possible. It's a release of ownership back to them. In the ideal conference, the student comes in with a handful of questions, and the teacher has a few. They have a conversation about where the work is and where they want it to go. But we have to listen. Listening in the conference means students are talking, and it's not just in response to our questions. It's us leaning in and taking notes on what they are saying.

Your notes should be your breadcrumbs, a reminder that the conference is really a dialogue. Ask students to have an idea of where they'd like to go with the piece and how you can help them get there. Tell them what you hear instead of making presumptions.

When the dialogue feels more delightful and rigorous, the writing then feels more authentic. You become the audience that the writer is wondering about and writing for. Audience gives writers some purpose and helps them think about what it means to communicate with that audience: what they need to hear, what emotions they like to elicit, and how best to do that. The more authentic the assignment—and the more it's based on student interest and student choice—the more authentic written voices the student can cultivate. The more the student feels engaged, the more they feel ownership over the assignment and will be active participants in the conference. Self-assessment is the driving force, but at its core, assessment is dialogue.

Formative assessment should come together as a collaboration. The more we hear from students—what they see and what questions they have—the more our assessment helps them along the path they want to take. This is a much healthier way for teachers to engage with students overall. It feels better in every way. It doesn't feel as didactic. It's not punitive. The feedback is actually desired because the goal is to make the composition better, not to try to find fault with it.

When you make assessment a conversation instead of a judgment and work with students to address progress, these experiences will become more student-centered and low-stakes. When we've mini-mized the language of evaluation and ask students what their vision is, revision is seen as a privilege rather than a punishment. Use rubrics to show your students what you are looking for, and talk with parents and caregivers about how story relates to the progress of their children's written work.

Whereas rubrics are normally very outcome-based, what you build into a rubric is a process (see Figure 5.1). What we need to do is honor the effort in the writing process and affirm those inputs as much as we affirm the final piece on the rubric. If a student provides

Figure 5.1
POWER OF STORY RUBRIC

Authenticity	Does this feel like you? Is it motivated by a personal purpose? What is the purpose of your writing?
Voice	Tone, expression, mood, impact on the audience
Elements	Character, setting, plot, beginning, climax, ending
Craft	Meaningful repetition, white space, punctuation, use of longer and shorter sentences, use of art
Language and Translanguaging	Use of home language, facility between English and the home language
Audience Considerations	Who is this for? What is the purpose? What is the impact you want to have on your reader?
Vocabulary	Matching to mood and purpose, stretching to try new things
Grammatical Structures	Short and long sentences, paragraphing

elaboration and counterexamples and checks off more boxes on the rubric, that's fine. But we would like to augment our thinking about what process-oriented rubrics are versus outcome-oriented rubrics. Students will submit multiple questions to ask the teacher. Following that conversation, students will formulate and submit multiple revisions. Students might participate in writing workshops, peer groups, or other activities. We talk about the writing process, yet we grade the writing product.

We spend so little time with the final product relative to the process. Nonetheless, we evaluate the product. We have to figure out how to reward and evaluate the process, not just the product.

We really want our students to take the process seriously and wrestle with their work. There are effort-based approaches and ability-based approaches. Typically, we fall into ability. What we really need to do is demand and reward effort. The effort students put into their assignments are much more telling of what their experience will be like over the year than any individual outcome in September. Whether we continue to call them *rubrics* or *frameworks*, the building blocks must be focused on process more than outcome.

Best Practice Guidelines for Excellence in Conferring

Listen Deeply and Be Intentional with Your Questions

Let us rally around the idea that stories need receiving; they need open hands and open hearts from all the adults in the room. Turn off your own personal distractions and be present. Ask your students to be present too. Talk about what it will take to make that happen. Put aside screen and paper if you are in-person and listen. If you are virtual, listen deeply; don't multitask. Put aside your personal emails; try to turn down the volume of your own life and up the volume of your student's story. Open-ended, genuine questions asked out of curiosity will stimulate the student's imagination and creativity, and it will establish a pattern of communication between you and the student that is based in authentic, caring, and curious interactions. This leads to deep, long-lasting bonds and helps extract maximum enjoyment and minimize danger and damage because you established a well-trod communication routine.

Always remember—in all situations where you interact with students—that every student wants to succeed. They are almost never actually "lazy" or "unmotivated." They are far more likely to be insecure, anxious, and afraid. Students are much more likely to engage with you as themselves when they know that you hear them and are listening to them.

When teaching writing to a student or working with them to become more skilled at writing, *never ask a question that you already know the answer to.* This goes contrary to how we often interact with children and requires a tremendous amount of self-awareness and self-monitoring on the part of the teacher. But we guarantee you that the rewards of following this rule are monumental and unimaginably wonderful. We tend as teachers to ask rhetorical questions. We can try to counter this with an intentional practice around our genuine interest in our students' stories or ask questions that are harder to answer *yes* or *no* to. Take 5–10 seconds to count yourself into a more inquiry-based stance, and let your students know you are going to do this to avoid asking what you already know or receiving what predetermined response you want them to give.

When considering grammar and structure, our students must become familiar with 26 different symbols (i.e., the alphabet), which often follow rules that are difficult to understand. Spelling is eccentric and varied, and pronunciation is no better. There are numerous exceptions to almost all the "rules." But this is all part of the joy of language learning, and by writing and crafting narratives, we can help our students come to love the structure and eccentricity of language usage as something not to be feared, but to be embraced.

Remember that the entire point of grammar is to ensure that we have agreed-upon rules of written and oral communication so that we have the best chance of understanding each other correctly and not misinterpreting the ideas and intent of one another.

Truly, is it any wonder that learning to write is a very daunting task? Think of the magnitude of processing and synthesizing what needs to be done even to write down the word *boy*, be able to say it, and know what it means.

We would imagine that many of you will see the logic in this, and it will resonate with your own life experience and feelings. But there still will be a question in your minds, especially since you are teachers, along the lines of "But isn't the Socratic method and other methods of questioning in which the questioner knows the answer but asks anyway a very valid method of instruction?" And the answer to that is yes, for the interrogator is not looking for a particular answer from a student but is attempting to engage in an inquisitive dialogue designed to train the student's mind to undergo a particular process of analysis. The goal is not to get the student to say a particular thing but to engage in a method of inquiry to understand particular issues, ideas, hypotheses, and historical inquiry.

Much more common, though, is the practice of asking students specific questions to quiz them to check comprehension of the lesson or concept being taught to them. When we are checking for understanding, this is fine, as the student understands that this is in the nature of a quiz or information check. All the feelings of distress associated with being quizzed will be present, but that is OK in this case because we are actually and intentionally asking these questions to verify comprehension.

And it is the same with writing. Inquiry-based questions are always critical and the best way to center all our deepest listening.

- What felt good about your writing today?
- What felt hard?

- What would you like to be able to do with this story you are working on?
- Who is the audience you are writing for?
- What aspect of the mechanics of writing feel challenging, and how can I help?
- Tell me more about your story. What feels inspiring for you in this story?
- What are you learning about yourself by writing this story?
- What craft element would you like to show me or that you would like more help on?
- What is your best-case outcome?
- What would you like someone to feel from this? Or learn from this?
- I am curious: How do you get from here to there in where you want to go?
- I am learning about you, and your writing helps me understand you. What would you like your audience to understand, and how can I help you get there?

Intentional Notetaking

Notetaking itself is a form of assessment. We can use our notes to look back and forth in the lives of our students as writers. Also, it is very powerful for your students to see you honor their work and stories with your notetaking. Weekly reviews of notes can help you see the progress your students are making in these areas, and you can use these categories as structures for how you take notes each time you meet so your students can find the conferences predictable and come prepared to talk with you. Each of the following areas can be done as a single, separate conference to home in on specific areas of their writing, but you can also do a conference that touches on each of these areas if you want to do a thorough read-through of a piece.

Storytelling Strengths and Audience

Let your students watch you record their oral storytelling in a conference. Ask them what mood and tone they are going for. Have them know that storytelling is a valuable tool for writing by taking it seriously enough to take notes on it. Let them know you are curious about stories they return to again and again, stories that inspire their emotion, or stories they are excited to tell. When we sat beside one student, and she was struggling to express a strong emotion she felt in a conversation with her mother about their journey here in the United States, we could ask her, "What is it in this story that resonates for you in a bigger way? Talk to me about that, and then I can help you illuminate that."

Idea Development

Ask your students to work with you to expand ideas right there in the conference by asking them open-ended questions. "What more can you say about your story? Can you use details or art to show us the mood, tone, or humor of this experience?" Take notes on what they say and let them know you will be circling back to them either virtually with an online document or in person to follow up on how they expanded their ideas in this piece. When one of our students sat with us writing for the first time, putting letters on the page or screen, they may not have been perfect, but they were his marks on the page. He said, "This is a story about my mom and me at the park." We could use the arts and visuals we have talked about earlier in this book to help him have a moment of quiet and caring communication when he could draw or sketch or tell us something wonderful about that day in the park, something he may have needed those tools to expand that idea. And the revelation comes with us, right there, in that seminal moment.

Strategy and Craft

Work with your student to connect the story to a genre as the way to share their story. Revisit the structures of narrative we discussed in Chapter 3. Help them have a conversation with you about this, such as, "What structure are you using to tell your story today? Why did you make that choice?" or, "Let's try a new structure here to mix things up a bit," or, "Let's take a look at some of the old and new structures that might fit this story and help get it ready for an audience." Bring books and mentor texts with you to the strategy conference. If you know your student is working on a particular genre, bring that style of book. Share excerpts of those texts where you see possible craft elements: strong character descriptions, an evocative beginning or ending, good punctuation and grammar, and creative use of white space. One of our students came to the conference with a story that felt so plain, she was worried her audience (of friends) wouldn't like it all that much. We showed her Carmen Agra Deedy's book *The Rooster Who Would Not Be Quiet!* to share the ways the author uses punctuation in delightful ways, and we invited her to try the same in her story.

Revision

For an expert storyteller, revision feels like polishing a jewel, but for the storyteller in practice, writing and revision can be really hard. Every single change is a hardship for a writer who has worked to get even those few words on the page or screen. Be sensitive to this in this part of a conference or, if this is a separate conference, even more so. It always helps to center that feeling with an acknowledgment, such as, "I know it feels hard to change words or parts of a story when you have been working so hard on it, but I promise all writers feel this little pang. We can use this section you delete somewhere else, later. For any good writer, nothing really ever goes to waste!"

You can have your student reread a piece to you, which is truly the best technique for revision there is. And for us, as a community of storytellers, it will feel like home for your students to come back around to the oral stories again! Have them do this while they are on the screen or with their pen on the page so they can make changes as they read it to you. You can also interject here, saying, "Hm, that sentence feels like it will be more powerful if it is shorter; can you take a look to see how we can break up that longer sentence?" Try to contextualize changes with them as writer to writer, with the idea that they are preparing for a real audience.

Reflection

We want students to walk away with a better understanding of their work and an idea of what immediate and actionable next steps they can do for their writing. We also want them to leave with a sense of affirmation that they're moving in the right direction and that there is value in what they're doing. We want students to leave with a set of directives and a sense of renewed purpose and energy. We love when the students are nearly jogging back to their work just to get writing, as opposed to slumping back in defeat. We want them to be in conversation with us via technology or in person as often as we can about their writing. Conferences are relational. They are about you and the student. Take time at the end of the conference for a "playback." Reiterate what you did together, what you heard the student say, and how you appreciate their time. Give your time together a moment to reflect. Your students won't think that is silly or small. They will understand and remember that you valued this time with them.

Students want to be affirmed, but they also want to be challenged. Affirmation is taking the work seriously at every age. And we want to motivate the students early on to develop a desire for feedback because feedback means that people are taking you seriously. They want to leave also knowing that they're involved in serious work. From the earliest ages through high school, to know that you are having a serious writing conference with a grown-up—that someone is taking this seriously—is memorable. They will feel a great sense of excitement that it's worthwhile to continue working on this piece. And they will want to keep doing it, because writing is not something that happens in isolation; they have changed you with their work, they will change someone else (their audience), and they will grow as writers.

6

Student Writers
as World Changers

The researcher and scholar Rudine Sims Bishop has transformed the landscape of reading with her seminal work on "mirrors, windows, and doors," speaking to how our students must be able to see themselves in the pages of a text. They must be able to see their beautiful souls, sense of self, and identity. In order to have power, you must see that you belong at every table. Bishop (1990) said, "Literature transforms human experience and reflects it back to us, and in that reflection we can see our own lives and experiences as part of the larger human experience."

This is true for writing too. If our students are constantly being told to conform to existing old forms of narrative, that is a form of authority that is stifling. The idea we have proposed of reading as "breathing in" and writing as "breathing out" is true of this idea too: we cannot be dedicated to a wide variety and diversity of what our students read and then, when they go to write, pull them back into the same very narrow places. We have to help our students see that their own writing forms, styles, and voices have a very important place in the world and in world changing.

Dr. Uri Hanson, neuroscientist and researcher at Princeton, has demonstrated through brain scans that a storyteller's words affect the brain activity of the listeners (Mohi ud Din, n.d.). Words and stories can stimulate neural coupling, where the same regions of the brain can be activated from the teller to the listener. Stories of certain structures can trigger the release of oxytocin, which is associated with connection and even empathy. Depending on the story, it could even release cortisol, a stress hormone.

This research demonstrates the power of social networks, and we create those networks by sharing narratives. "Stories require us to accept that all of us possess the ability to change."

To get people who are writing to see themselves as writers is a transformational move. Kids know they have to write, but they don't all see themselves as writers or storytellers. When we shift the instruction so it's really about identities, we help our students see that they are always growing and changing; this is a matter of survival and success. The messaging becomes "we are writers here and we value your voice." When we move from separate exercises that are just about getting better at writing and toward really seeing ourselves as proficient storytellers who use our writing skills to tell better stories, that's world changing. The world changing is apparent when the kid you never hear from is all of a sudden reading their poem on stage.

A community where people feel like they belong is a community where people know their voices matter. When we cultivate a space rooted in this principle, students are finally able to communicate in their entire linguistic repertoire. Creating a classroom culture that suspends judgment and prioritizes kindness, engaged listening, and collaboration allows students to be vulnerable, see themselves as valuable, and think and write critically. Once we have established a community of belonging, we must consistently prioritize student voice so storytelling can happen naturally. Some tangible ways to show your students their voices are valued in the classroom are to reconceptualize the modes of story, showcase vulnerability, and give students a variety of prompts.

To cultivate storytelling as natural, it is essential to reconceptualize story in a more organic way at younger and younger ages. The modes of production in school are normally teacher-facing, which often means the types of stories students feel comfortable sharing are extremely limited. For them, it often doesn't make any sense to tell a story they'd typically share with friends if you're writing it down for a teacher. With this in mind, our mission is not just asking kids what stories they have but giving them meaningful outlets for all types of stories. We can harness the structures of social media (the short burst of an idea that comes from Twitter inspiration, the combination of video and narration that comes from TikTok, and the image-based storytelling that comes from Instagram). When students of all ages can be ethnographers of all types of stories, it will be natural for them to collect the stories that surround them in their community and want to share these stories with others.

We live in absolutely, unimaginably magical times. Our students can tell stories without having to physically write them down. For those who have great difficulty writing, this is a life-changing gift. For those who are comfortable with writing, this is an added benefit to open new and varied ways of telling their stories.

Writing is still how our society transmits most of its stories. It is a tried-and-true method. Many members of society are familiar with it, comfortable with it, and expecting it as the vehicle for how they will receive information. And it goes without saying that facility and comfort with written communication are essential tools in the workplace. And so this book is indeed about writing. But keep in mind, always, that this is a book about writing as a way to be a storyteller. And the real thing that we are trying to teach our students, the real skill we are trying to give them, the real freedom we want them to be able to create for themselves, is to be a storyteller.

Natural storytelling is encouraged with curriculum that celebrates what is important to our students. Storytelling that exists in comics, film, social media platforms, or other mediums should not only exist outside the classroom. To see kids in the 21st century doing the things that they like to do and talking about the things they like to talk about in the stories on your classroom bookshelf yields a very different kind of response. Contemporary authors create characters and stories that are accessible, relatable, and have a real impact on kids. They see their life and their experiences reflected back to them, or they see really beautiful artwork in picture books, and they get charged up about that. When kids are excited, they start to write better. It's important to find a healthy tension between reading stories that make you feel known and reading stories that make you feel like you know other people. Kids need stories that expand their horizons *as well* as stories that affirm the power of their own local narratives.

Let's ask all our students, "If you could change the world, what's one thing you would change? If you had the power to share any message, what message would you share?" A huge part of helping kids open up about these questions is helping them be vulnerable and brave in the classroom setting. You tell them they can be vulnerable and take risks through several different methods.

Honor Mistakes as a Step Toward Growth

When we sit beside Carlita and notice she has put periods at the end of every word in her story, then gently try to show her that periods go at the end of a sentence, and she says with surprise, "I knew *that*. I just *love* periods!" we know we have to stop ourselves and really think about what we are referring to as "mistakes" and how to be more open to the idea of mistakes as "attempts." Say to Carlita, "I love that you love periods!" Have confidence that she will shed some of her joy and become just like everyone else soon enough, which is both happy and a little bit sad. Sometimes the mistakes our students make are also intentional if we see them in the context of their home language. And in these cases, the "mistakes" are absolutely profoundly brilliant.

Honor the Perspectives They Bring

Everyone comes from a different background, family story, and experience. When we are celebratory of that, we can help our students to be truly themselves. If they are used to being part of a huge family at home, they will tell a story about family in a different way than we would. If we stop and listen with care, we will learn a lot from them.

Create Norms for When There Is a Disagreement

"Yes, and. . . ." "I want to add on to what you are saying, even though we are going in different directions." Writing stories together means we might sometimes have a different way of tackling a subject as personal as family or as broad as life. Give students sentence stems as a pathway to have caring conversations when things feel tough. When a student said, "Yes, and . . ." during a debate with a writing partner about their differing experiences, we saw the partner lean in, interested, simply because she used the word *and* and not *but*.

Celebrate and Publish Student Writing

Display student writing on classroom walls, post them online, or send the work home regularly so they can share finished products with grandparents, parents, and caregivers. Celebrations really forge bonds between all our student writers and help them become less judgmental of themselves and others when they see us cheering them on.

Create ways for students to celebrate one another's stories by giving badges online or offline and celebrating the small things. "I liked the way your writing ended. I liked how I felt when I listened to your story."

Create Time for Reflection

"How did your writing go today? How did your story feel for you today?" Let this reflection be shared in partners or with larger groups through online technology too. By reflecting together, our students become less fearful that they've made mistakes. One of our students said, "When I saw that Raul did the same topic as I did, and did it so differently, that made me excited to try it his way next time."

When we celebrate the small steps of writing and storytelling in the classroom and leave time for students to reflect on that, all the members of that community feel their contributions are valued, which helps them take risks in vulnerability. And vulnerability is necessary to become a strong writer.

Here are some ways to get your students writing in ways that feel vulnerable, powerful, and world-changing:

- Write out a list of your students' favorite words in different languages, including mother tongues in local communities. Then write a story or tell a story together mixing the languages. Don't be afraid to try new sounds and have your students use sound and language to create their own language as they tell their stories.

- Imagine a world with one universal language. Tell a story about it.

- Talk and write about the strong emotions you have about the world around you. For example, start with anger. Try fear. Experiment with joy. Connect that one emotion to something happening in the world and write about it.

- Think of an artifact you cherish and love. Write about who you would give it to and why.

- Start with the words "As a world-changer, I . . ." or "As a world-changer, we. . . ."

In the book *Fireflies* by Julie Brinckloe, a little boy is eating dinner at dusk when he notices a firefly in his backyard. He rushes out with a jar in his hand and soon collects a multitude of them. The little boy is filled with wonder. He feels he is holding a piece of the moon in his hands. But soon he realizes that in order for the fireflies to thrive they must be free. He is overcome with sadness. He must choose between his desire to capture the fireflies with what he knows he must do. They fly away into the night sky. The little boy is happy knowing he has done the right thing. Brinckloe's message is one of compassion and care.

The youngest children understand the magnitude of generosity and giving. In Jacqueline Woodson's beautiful book *The Other Side*, two girls choose to be friends despite the racial barriers established by society and others that are between them. The story is set in a segregated town divided by a fence. Clover, who is Black, lives near the fence and wonders about her mother's warning to never climb over it because it is not safe on the other side. Annie is white; she has been given the same confusing warning from her mother. The girls start out by watching each other from afar, but as the long days of summer quietly pass, they grow curious and begin to get to know each other. Clover and Annie spend many days sitting on the fence together, talking and laughing and becoming friends. Though Clover's friends are initially bewildered to see her sitting together with her new friend, all the children begin to jump rope together, and when they need a rest, they perch together on the fence. Woodson gives agency to her child characters to tell their own story, presenting a child's story of curiosity leading to friendship and friendship leading to a hopeful future.

These authors share worlds in which children's own decisions are powerful and lifechanging. In *The Dreamer* by Pam Muñoz Ryan, she shares a fictionalized version of the poet Pablo Neruda's childhood. Neftali finds an outlet for the magic he senses and takes on the pseudonym Pablo Neruda. The narrative of Neruda shows us that anything is possible with imagination to guide us. Ask your students these questions and have them write about them:

- Inhabit a character you admire from history. Tell a story from their perspective.
- Create an imaginary character you believe can change the world.
- Write a beginning, middle, and end of a story with a strong character who changes the community in some crucial way.
- Write a superhero story with an urgent problem the world needs to solve.

In the book *Fox* by Margaret Wild, Dog rescues Magpie from a forest fire, but her wing is badly injured. She will never fly again, and Dog has been blinded. At first Magpie is tempted to succumb to her own grief, but Dog tends to her and the two become friends. Magpie rides on Dog's back acting as his missing eyes and feeling the rush of wind under her wings as if she were flying once more. From sorrow and grief come transformation and transcendence.

Ask your students to picture an ending to the most beautiful story they can imagine: of themselves, their community, or the world. Now write about it or tell a story about it. Let us all hear it and know it.

We often think of kindness as a "soft skill," one that is a supplement to learning but not really about learning itself. But in truth, the human spirit depends on kindness for sustenance. Building ways to tell stories in our classrooms, write them down, and share them is a way to create a kindness curriculum. We are teaching students to listen, really listen, and show the greatest of all kindnesses: be present to another's story. This is the first and best step to world changing: be present for another human being. From there, we can use the stories we read and the stories we write as a blueprint for how to treat others in the world.

We must start with kindness to oneself and then to one's community if we want to empower ourselves to want to change the world.

World changing begins early. The youngest child listening to the stories of the classroom learns that tenderness is what will make it possible to reach out to an elder, a friend, or a stranger. The middle schooler or high school student knows that tenderness is what makes it possible to empathize with those who are at risk or victims of a systemic injustice. They have seen this in the books they have read and the stories they write. We are all human, after all. We are more connected than we sometimes realize. Stories are what builds empathy. As we have said here in these chapters, the stories our children write are the stories of loss and of being found. Together let's go forward in this complex world with the simplicity of knowing what kindness really is and making it our mantra for teaching writing and learning together.

Conclusion: Two Key Ingredients

When we give students the space and an attentive audience—when we give them ways to share what is important to them, what they love, how they are loved, how they love and care about others, or about the things and ideas in the world that mean something to them—almost anyone can be a good storyteller. Most of the kids who matriculate through school are able to write down everything they can say. The problem is that we don't necessarily connect writing with storytelling. Part of transforming the power of writing and making it accessible to all is to take it off its unnecessary throne and put it back down along with the everyday skills of literacy, like speaking and listening. Storytelling is normal and natural, and we all do it.

In order to create spaces for powerful stories, we must allow the stories that are inside all of us to get out. It's not as though there's some magic thing we have to do. It's really about creating spaces where people feel heard, where people feel valued, where their ideas are taken into consideration, where we slow things down, where we're really sensitive audience members, and where we take big ideas outside the classroom and into the world.

Teaching writing is a channel by which we can show our students how to produce text and be active problem solvers in a world that needs our helping hands . . . and voices.

Technology has changed the modality of story, and there's no question that it has allowed many more people to be able to share stories with larger and larger networks of people. With social media, story is iterative, shaped and reshaped by multiple tellers. Story through technology is not without its challenges, but it is empowering for everyday people. That is why we have to envision a teaching environment where attention to the power of storytelling in writing is not limited to literature but exists in every single genre and every single place: in the smallest spaces of breath, on a Twitter feed, in the moment you meet someone, in the last days you share with a beloved grandmother, or in a text message to a cherished friend. The way story gets conveyed is constantly changing. By the time we publish this book, there will be more ways to share stories than we ever could imagine or articulate in this instant. But that is the beauty of the power of story; it is the one timeless thing we can count will never change. It's been with us since the beginning.

We aim to teach our students that there are two things they need to grow to be an extraordinary writer, learner, thinker, citizen, and friend. These two things are really good at adapting to whatever the state of literacy is at any point in history. They are impervious to time and personality and oppression. If they are used well, they have the power to free people and prevent silencing. These two things will give every single human a chance to affect society for the better and to use whatever those new technologies and tools are to keep our humanity going.

These two ingredients are love and story.

Students can't just be receivers of knowledge; they have to also be producers of it. The one thing every child brings with them to class and everywhere they go is stories. They are the greatest power a child has, if given the chance to use them, to be known and to learn well. As educators, we can accomplish all our goals and see our students achieve great things if we let stories guide the way with love. We are not oversimplifying this. We have seen it with our own eyes time and time again. By listening to stories and by leaning into love, our students can become truly empowered by their own stories and cherish one another's. When they do this, they are fortified for all their next steps in the world, for whatever they will need stories for. Stories are their shields, their courage, their superpowers.

At the start of this book, we shared our principles and values for creating a roadmap to a lifetime of story: to center joy in your teaching, to listen deeply, to value wonder, to promote creative innovation in our students' own ideas, to help them become problem solvers with the use of storytelling, to value empathy as a core value for the power of story, to build routines that honor student voice, to help our students thrive independently with structures that encourage them to try, and to constantly and authentically celebrate the small and big steps as our students become powerful storytellers.

These ideas follow us through this book, but we want to gather you in one more moment to talk about what we mean by celebration and remind us together why it is important. Celebration is our beginning, and it is our ending. When we first started teaching writing, we set aside one day a month for writing celebrations. A district we worked with took this very seriously; the parents would dress their children in their semiformal clothing, and the grandparents offered to bring in food. It was always a moving, beautiful celebration of children's voices and the humble stories they told, their first marks in the world. The grandmothers would sit on the tiny chairs in the front of the room, their hands clasped, their eyes full of tears. Let the world be this way again; let these stories move us to tears. We need them.

Stories are always the wind at our students' backs, the sun shining upon them after a rainstorm, the blue skies ahead of them as they move toward hopes and dreams for the rest of their lives. Keeping their ancestors with them, their languages, their elders, the stories they make by being alive and amazing in this world—this is what they carry forward.

Know this: Your own legacy will be in the stories your students tell, write, and share for the rest of their lives and all the ways they move toward their own hopes and dreams. Someday they will ask their own loved ones, "What is the story you want to tell?" And they will lean in and deeply listen, just like you did. This is what lasts. This is what matters.

Acknowledgments

We would like to thank the great team at ASCD for their stellar support, insight, and wisdom throughout the creation of this book. A special thanks to Susan Hills, who started this journey with us and coached us toward a big goal, and to Megan Doyle, for championing our ideas with a graceful touch and making them better. Thanks to all the many people who helped bring this book to fruition, including Christopher Logan, Shajuan Martin, Circle Graphics, and for a special cover design, Jennifer Knotts.

A big thanks to Lisa DiMona and The Writer's House team for taking such good care of us as a writing team. Thanks to Paige Heimark for always saying yes with courage and for making this story work fun and deeply meaningful. To Cyrilla Ray: Cyr, you brought your clarity of thinking and your tender care for the life-changing magic of stories to support us in this project. Thanks to Sage Kashner, Arianna Carriel, Ashley Church, and Esther Seo for your fine and insightful attention to detail.

From Pam: To Jim, my true love, for creating the story of our lives, love story, work story, family story. For Mom, Cindy, Skip, Katie, Charlotte, Aaron, and now Gus: It is my greatest joy to accompany you all in your stories. Thank you, Ernest, for our beautiful friendship, for being a person of integrity and goodness in a world where we so need that, and for your true and powerful leadership in the work on behalf of children every day.

From Ernest: To my mom and dad, my first teachers and lifelong K–12 educators, for the daily examples you offered of goodness and greatness. To Jodene, Amani, Antonio, and Tripp for the daily joy and inspiration. To all of my students through the past 30 years for your curiosity, your passion, your genius, your stories, and your belief in me. And to Pam for your tireless ethic, your vision, and your unwavering support for children and families. It is the joy of my professional life to walk with you.

References

Adichie, C. N. (2009, July). The danger of a single story. TEDGlobal. https://www.ted.com/talks/chimamanda_ngozi_adichie_the_danger_of_a_single_story

Bell, C. (2014). *El deafo*. Harry N. Abrams.

Bishop, R. S. (1990). Mirrors, windows, and sliding glass doors. *Perspectives: Choosing and Using Books for the Classroom, 6*(3).

Brinckloe, J. (1986). *Fireflies*. Aladdin Books.

Deedy, C. A. (2017). *The rooster who would not be quiet!* Scholastic.

Flett, J. (2021). *We all play*. Greystone Kids.

Hall, D. (1983). *Ox-cart man*. Puffin.

Haring, K. (2010). *Keith Haring journals* (Penguin Classics Deluxe Edition). Penguin.

Heard, G. (2016). *Heart maps*. Heinemann.

Hurston, Z. N. (1990). *Their eyes were watching god*. HarperCollins.

Johnson, L. (2020). *You should see me in a crown*. Scholastic.

Koenitz, H., Di Pastena, A., Jansen, D., de Lint, B., & Moss, A. (2018). The myth of "universal" models. In *Interactive Storytelling* (pp. 107–120). Springer.

Maillard, K. N. (2019). *Fry bread: A Native American family*. Roaring Brook.

Mohi ud Din, M. (n.d.). How connecting neuroscience, storytelling, and psychology can create measurable impact for refugee youth. UNHCR. https://www.unhcr.org/innovation/connecting-neuroscience-storytelling-psychology-can-create-measurable-impact-refugee-youth/

Morales, Y. (2021). *Bright star*. Neal Porter Books.

Myers, W. D. (1996). *Brown angels: An album of pictures and verse*. HarperCollins.

O'Neill, S. P. (2013, January/December). Translating oral literature in Indigenous societies: Ethnic aesthetic performances in multicultural and multilingual settings. *Journal of Folklore Research, 50*(1–3), 217–250.

Paley, V. G. (1990). *The boy who would be a helicopter*. Harvard University Press.

Paley, V. G. (1981). *Wally's stories*. Harvard University Press.

Paley, V. G. (1979). *White teacher*. Harvard University Press.

Paul, B., & Paul, M. (2021). *Peace*. NorthSouth Books.

Phillips Collection. (2022). Jacob Lawrence: The migration series. https://lawrencemigration.phillipscollection.org/

Reynolds, J. (2021). *Stuntboy, in the meantime*. Simon & Schuster.

Reynolds, J. (2019). *Look both ways: A tale told in ten blocks*. Atheneum Books.

Ryan, P. M. (2012). *The dreamer*. Scholastic.

Scott, J., Douris, R., & Junod, K. (2021, July 19). On "Outside Child," Allison Russell confronts trauma with compassion. *NPR*. https://www.npr.org/sections/world-cafe/2021/07/19/1017881727/on-outside-child-allison-russell-confronts-trauma-with-compassion

Shapiro, E. (2021, August 30). It's critical that the rivers continue to flow: Environmental activist Nicole Horseherder on reclaiming water rights for Native Americans. *Time*. https://time.com/6093093/water-rights-nicole-horseherder/

Sium, A., & Ritskes, E. (2013). Speaking truth to power: Indigenous storytelling as an act of living resistance. *Decolonization: Indigeneity, Education & Society, 2*(1), ii–x.

Srinivasan, D. (2021). *What I am*. Viking Books.

Susag, D. M. (1998). *Roots and branches: A resource of Native American literature—Themes, lessons, and bibliographies*. NCTE.

Travers, P. L. (2018). *Mary Poppins*. Houghton Mifflin Harcourt.

Travers P. L. (1976). The world of the hero. *Parabola Myth and the Quest for Meaning, 1*(1).

White, E. B. (2015). *Charlotte's web*. HarperCollins.

Whiteduck, M. (2013). But it's our story. Read it: Stories my grandfather told me and writing for continuance. *Decolonization: Indigeneity, Education & Society, 2*(1).

Wild, M. (2006). *Fox*. Kane/Miller.

Willems, M. (2004). *Knuffle bunny: A cautionary tale*. Hyperion.

Woodson, J. (2014). *Brown girl dreaming*. Puffin.

Woodson, J. (2001). *The other side*. Nancy Paulsen Books.

Yang. K. (2018). *Front desk*. Arthur A. Levine Books.

Index

The letter *f* following a page locator denotes a figure.

art
  everyday, 50–51
  in the making of writers, 39–40
  visual, 51–53
artifacts, 1–2, 12
art stations, 40
assessment
  of authenticity, 102–103
  conferring in, 103–106
  formative, 105
  powerful, 104
  of quality, 103
  rubrics in, 106–107, 106*f*
assessment, best practice
  guidelines for conferring
    on idea development, 111–112
    listen deeply, 107–110
    notetake intentionally, 110–111

  question intentionally, 107–110
  reflect, 113–114
  on revision, 112–113
  on storytelling strengths and
    audience, 111
  on strategy and craft, 112
assignments, creating community
  through, 28–29
audience
  conferring about, 111
  connecting with, 43

Basquiat, Jean Michel, 51
Belle, Cece, 91–93
Black and White Contrasts, 55
brain, stories and the human, 116
Bright Star (Morales), 86–88
Build a World activity, 22

cameras, using, 40
Cartoons, writing story with, 56–57
celebration
    to build communities of
        belonging, 34–35, 100
    meaning of, 127
    methods of, 119
Change the World with Objects, 22
character, in C-SAW method, 64–66
circular structure, 67–68
Classroom Redecoration, 22
Comics, writing story with, 40,
    56–57
communities of belonging,
    building through
        creating community norms,
            28–29
        deadlines, 29
        environment, 13–14, 28
        feedback, 29
        reconceptualizing story, 11–12,
            42–43
        self-kindness and self-empathy,
            33
        self-worth, 12–14
        short, fast assignments, 28–29
        storyteller commitments
            banners, 28–29
        structured independent writing,
            30–31
        tools and inspiration, 27–28
        valuing voice, 116–117
        writing block, addressing, 33
communities of belonging,
    building through activities
        Build a World activity, 22
        Change the World with Objects,
            22
        Classroom Redecoration, 22

Community Animals, 17
Daily Writing, 26–27
Innovation Hub, 22
Learning Empathy, 25–26
Letters of Introduction, 25
Listening Deeply, 18–19
Maker Space, 22
Meditation Moments, 32
Our Story Soup, 16
Power of Story days, 34
Ritual, 33
A Smooth Stone, 16
Using Sound, 32
Wondering Journal, 20
Wondering Partners, 20
Wonder Jar, 19–20
Wonder Window, 19
"Yes and" Throw a Party, 16–17
communities of belonging,
    principles of building
        be pro-empathy, 24–26, 99
        celebrate, 34–35, 100
        center joy, 14–17, 98
        create routines, 26–29, 99
        disrupt negative thinking,
            31–33, 100
        foster problem solving, 22–24,
            99
        help students to thrive
            independently, 29–31, 99
        listen deeply, 17–19, 98–99
        prioritize creativity, 20–22, 99
        value wonder, 19–20, 99
        welcome innovation, 20–22, 99
Community Animals, 17
company, stories as, 6
creativity, prioritizing, 20–22, 99
C-SAW story creation, 64–65
culture, popular, 51

darkness and the light, 2
deadlines, 29
Deaf culture, 52–53, 75
disagreement, create norms for,
    119

El Deafo (Bell), 91–93
empathy, learning and valuing,
    24–26, 33, 99
empowerment, 5–6
environment
    building communities of
        belonging, 13–14, 28
    of wonder, building, 19–20
event-centered structure, 75

feedback, 29
Finish this Story exercise, 38
frameworks, flexible, 63
Front Desk (Yang), 88–90
Fry Bread (Maillard), 84–86

graphic novel templates, 40

Haring, Keith, 50–51
Heart Maps, 54–55
hero's journey, 73–74

idea development, assessing, 111–112
innovation, valuing, 20–22, 99
Innovation Hub, 22
inspiration, building community
    through, 27–28

Johnson, Leah, 95–98
joy, centering, 14–17, 33, 61, 98

kindness, 33, 122–123
Kishotenketsu, 74
Knuffle Bunny (Willems), 82–84

Lawrence, Jacob, 53–54
Letters of Introduction, 25
light and the darkness, 2
linear structure, 63–67
listen deeply, 17–19, 98–99, 107–110
listening corners, 17–19
LitWorld, 4
Look Both Ways (Reynolds), 93–95
love, guiding the way with, 126–127

Maillard, Kevin Noble, 84–86
Maker Space, 22
Maps of the Heart, 54–55
Meditation Moments, 32
mentor lessons, crafting, 98–100
mentors, visual artists as, 53–54
mentor texts
    first to second grades, 84–86
    fourth to sixth grades, 88–90
    high school, 95–98
    kindergarten, 82–84
    second to fourth grades, 86–88
    sixth grade, 91–95
    using, 79–82
mischiefmakers, 49
mistakes, honoring, 118–119
mo`olelo, 41
Morales, Yuyi, 86–88
Murals, 55

nature-centered structure, 74–75
negative thinking, disrupting,
    31–33, 100
notetaking
    in assessment, 110–111
    while listening, 17–19

oral storytelling
    audience, connecting with, 43
    creating belonging through,
        41–42

historically, 43
identity and, 47–49
interactive nature of, 44–45
into print, 45–46, 49–50
quiet voices, bringing out the,
    46–47
talk/listen/talk (TLT) loop, 38
valuing, 37
Our Story Soup, 16

partnerships, storytelling, 38
perspectives, honoring differing,
    119
picture making in the making of
    writers, 39–40
play in the making of writers, 39
Power of Story days, 34
power of story mentor lesson,
    98–100
problem solvers, becoming, 22–24,
    99
pro-empathy, core value of, 24–26,
    99
publish, 119

question intentionally, 107–110

recordings
    of dream stories, 29
    for listening, 17–19
    in partnership, 38
    putting words and letters
        together, 40
    as tools, 27
reflection
    in assessment, 113–114
    time for, 120–123
resistance narrative, 69–74
revision, assessing, 112–113
Reynolds, Jason, 93–95

ritual, using, 33
Robleto, 74
routines, creating, 26–29, 99

self, storifying, 42
self-kindness, 33
self-perception, changing, 12–14,
    41–42
Self-Portraits, 55
Silly Shape Stories, 57–58
simplicity, 65
Sketches, 55
A Smooth Stone, 16
social contract, entering the, 18
social media, story on, 44–45, 126
sound, using, 32
story
    cultivating, 102
    everyday, importance of, 50–51
    power of, 2–9, 125–128
storyteller commitments banners,
    28–29
storytellers, 62–63
storytelling. See also oral story-
    telling; visual storytelling
    collective, 44–45
    expectations, 76
    spiritual essence of, 62–63,
        76–77
    storyteller in, 62–63
    visual artists as mentors for,
        53–54
strategy and craft, assessing, 112
structured independent writing
    (SIW), 30–31
structures shaping story
    circular, 67–68
    event-centered, 75
    the hero's journey, 73–74
    importance of, 77

structures shaping story, (con't)
    linear, 63–67
    nature-centered, 74–75
    resistance/counterstructure,
        69–74
students, helping to thrive
    independently, 29–31, 99

talk/listen/talk (TLT) loop, 38
technology, story through, 126
tenderness, 123
Textures, writing story with, 56
tools, building community through,
    27–28

visual artists as mentors, 53–54
visual storytelling
    cultural resonance of, 51–53
    de-hierarchizing, 50–51
    valuing, 37
visual storytelling for writing
    Black and White Contrasts,
        55
    Cartoons, 56–57
    Comics, 56–57
    Maps of the Heart, 54–55
    Murals, 55
    Self-Portraits, 55
    Silly Shape Stories, 57–58
    Sketches, 55
    Textures, 56
voice
    empowering, 5
    quiet, bringing out the, 5
    valuing, 116–117
vulnerability, writers and, 120

wellness, story and, 7–8
Willems, Mo, 82–84

wonder
    building environments of, 19–20
    valuing, 99
Wondering Journal, 20
Wondering Partners, 20
Wonder Jar, 19–20
Wonder Window, 19
world changers, student writers as,
    115–123
writers, the making of
    art in, 39–40
    celebration in, 119
    confidence in, 46
    create norms for disagreement,
        119
    C-SAW method, 64–66
    empowering, voice in, 5
    identity in, 47–49
    instruction in, 116
    mistakes as a step toward
        growth in, 118–119
    perspectives, role in, 119
    picture making in, 39–40
    play in, 39
    publishing in, 119
    putting words and letters
        together, 40–41
    reflection time in, 120–123
    structure in, 59–62
    talk/listen/talk (TLT) loop, 38
    visual artists as mentors, 53–54
    vulnerability in, 120
writing block, addressing, 33
writing skills, improving, 6–7

Yang, Kelly, 88–90
"Yes and" Throw a Party, 16–17
You Should See Me in a Crown
    (Johnson), 95–98

About the Authors

**Pam Allyn** is an award-winning author, educator, and innovator. Her books include *Every Child a Super Reader*, coauthored with Dr. Ernest Morrell; *Your Child's Writing Life*, winner of the Mom's Choice Award; and *What to Read When*. She is a renowned public speaker and has created programs that achieve exceptional results in academics and well-being for students aged pre-K through grade 12. Her signature programs include LitCamp, LitLeague, and ReadyGen. Pam is the founder of many initiatives, including LitWorld, which champions the power of story worldwide, and Dewey, a family learning community to help caregivers learn, bond, and thrive. Pam is the creator, with her team at LitWorld, of World Read Aloud Day, celebrated in more than 60 countries each year. She was selected for the Laura Bush Fellowship for Women Leaders and Mentors and the Kellogg Foundation Fellowship for Racial Equity and Healing. Pam has received many honors for her work, including the James Patterson Page Turner Award, the Children's Village Legacy of Service Award, Scholastic's

Reading Champion Award, the Kent Williamson Leadership Award from the Conference on English Leadership, and the Columbia University Teachers College Distinguished Alumni Award.

 **Ernest Morrell** is an award-winning scholar, author, public speaker, researcher, and practitioner. He is the Coyle Professor of Literacy Education, a member of the faculty in the English and Africana Studies departments and director of the Center for Literacy Education at the University of Notre Dame. He is an elected Fellow of the American Educational Research Association, a past president of the National Council of Teachers of English (NCTE), and an elected member of the National Academy of Education. Ernest is also the recipient of the NCTE Distinguished Service Award, the Kent Williamson Leadership Award from the Conference on English Leadership, and the Divergent Award for Excellence in 21st Century Literacies. Ernest has authored 90 articles, research briefs, and book chapters and 10 scholarly monographs, including *Every Child a Super Reader*, coauthored with Pam Allyn; *Educating Harlem: A Century of Schooling and Resistance in a Black Community*; *Stories from Inequity to Justice in Literacy Education*; *New Directions in Teaching English*; and *Critical Media Pedagogy: Teaching for Achievement in City Schools*, which was awarded Outstanding Academic Title by *Choice* magazine of the American Library Association. Ernest has earned numerous commendations for his university teaching, including UCLA's Distinguished Teaching Award.

Related ASCD Resources

At the time of publication, the following resources were available (ASCD stock numbers in parentheses).

The Better Writing Breakthrough: Connecting Student Thinking and Discussion to Inspire Great Writing by Eleanor Dougherty, Laura Ann Billings, and Terry Roberts (#114010)

Engaging Students in Reading All Types of Text (Quick Reference Guide) by Monica Burns and Pam Allyn (#QRG121059)

Literacy Is Liberation: Working Toward Justice Through Culturally Relevant Teaching by Kimberly N. Parker (#122024)

The New Art and Science of Teaching Writing by Kathy T. Glass and Robert J. Marzano (#318145)

Reading, Writing, and Rigor: Helping Students Achieve Greater Depth of Knowledge in Literacy by Nancy Boyles (#118026)

Students Taking Action Together: 5 Teaching Techniques to Cultivate SEL, Civic Engagement, and a Healthy Democracy by Lauren M. Fullmer, Laura F. Bond, Crystal N. Molyneaux, Samuel J. Nayman, and Maurice J. Elias (#122029)

Teaching to Empower: Taking Action to Foster Student Agency, Self-Confidence, and Collaboration by Debbie Zacarian and Michael Silverstone (#120006)

Tools for Teaching Writing: Strategies and Interventions for Diverse Learners in Grades 3–8 by David Campos and Kathleen Fad (#114051)

For up-to-date information about ASCD resources, go to www.ascd.org. You can search the complete archives of *Educational Leadership* at www.ascd.org/el. To contact us, send an email to member@ascd.org or call 1-800-933-2723 or 703-578-9600.

WHOLE CHILD
TENETS

1 **HEALTHY**
Each student enters school healthy and learns about and practices a healthy lifestyle.

2 **SAFE**
Each student learns in an environment that is physically and emotionally safe for students and adults.

3 **ENGAGED**
Each student is actively engaged in learning and is connected to the school and broader community.

4 **SUPPORTED**
Each student has access to personalized learning and is supported by qualified, caring adults.

5 **CHALLENGED**
Each student is challenged academically and prepared for success in college or further study and for employment and participation in a global environment.

The ASCD Whole Child approach is an effort to transition from a focus on narrowly defined academic achievement to one that promotes the long-term development and success of all children. Through this approach, ASCD supports educators, families, community members, and policymakers as they move from a vision about educating the whole child to sustainable, collaborative actions.

Tell Your Story relates to the **engaged**, **supported**, and **challenged** tenets. *For more about the ASCD Whole Child approach, visit **www.ascd.org/wholechild**.*